The
Charity
Treasurer's
HANDBOOK

An introduction to voluntary sector
finance and accounting

3rd Edition

Gareth G. Morgan

DIRECTORY OF SOCIAL CHANGE

Published by
Directory of Social Change
24 Stephenson Way
London NW1 2DP
Tel: 08450 77 77 07; Fax: 020 7391 4804
email: publications@dsc.org.uk
www.dsc.org.uk
from whom further copies and a full publications catalogue are available.

Directory of Social Change Northern Office
Federation House, Hope Street, Liverpool L1 9BW
Policy & Research 0151 708 0136; email: research@dsc.org.uk

Directory of Social Change is a Registered Charity no. 800517

First published 2002
Second edition 2008
Third edition 2010

ISBN 978 1 906294 50 2

British Library Cataloguing in Publication Data
A catalogue record for this book is available from the British Library

Text and cover designed by Sarah Nicholson and Kate Bass
Typeset by Marlinzo Services, Frome
Printed and bound by Page Bros, Norwich

Disclaimer
This is an introductory book. It seeks to explain the framework of charity accounting, but it does not provide a full statement of the law. Where legal issues are covered, they are based on a summary of requirements as at 1 June 2010, but there could be subsequent changes. Many accounting concepts are presented at an overview level only (particularly in areas such as accruals accounting, charity taxation and production of final accounts under the Charities Statement of Recommended Practice (SORP). It is intended for guidance and is not a substitute for professional advice. No responsibility can be accepted by the publisher or author as a result of any person acting or refraining from acting on the basis of this publication.

Contents

About the series

This book is part of a series of starter guides aimed primarily at those who are new to the voluntary sector. The series is designed for people involved with charities or voluntary organisations or community groups of any size. All the titles offer practical, straightforward advice to enable readers to get the most out of their roles and responsibilities.

Also available in this series:
Charitable Status
Julian Blake
2008

The Charity Trustee's Handbook
Mike Eastwood
2001

Effective Fundraising
Luke FitzHerbert
2003

The Minute Taker's Handbook
Lee Comer and Paul Ticher
2002

For further information, please contact the Directory of Social Change (see page ii for details).

Also by Gareth G Morgan
The Charities Act 2006: A Guide for Foundations and Grant-Making Trusts in England and Wales (ACF 2007).

Preface

The aim of *The Charity Treasurer's Handbook* is to bring together many issues needed for effective accounting and financial management in UK charitable organisations, in a book which is short enough to be read in a few hours.

The role of treasurer, finance worker or finance manager in a voluntary organisation can be a rewarding one if it enables the organisation to achieve its aims. It need not be daunting, but it does require an appreciation of those issues that make the finances of charitable organisations different from businesses.

The *Handbook* will also be useful to those with financial experience in other sectors, who need a rapid overview of the accounting issues in a charity. The book is also intended for students on courses in charity and voluntary sector management, who need an appreciation of the requirements of financial management in the sector.

This book outlines some of the key issues of charity law that affect the work of treasurers and finance officers in smaller charities. It explains a range of terminology, such as restricted funds and the implications of the Charities Statement of Recommended Practice (SORP). It offers guidelines for day to day accounting procedures, as well as for year end accounts. It provides advice on issues such as appointing an auditor or independent examiner, and gives an overview of some of the specific tax issues affecting charities.

The approach does not seek to cover the full detail of every issue, but simply to give enough information so that the reader will understand the main requirements. It is hoped that this will enable a charity to make sensible decisions – and to enter into meaningful discussions with others when further guidance is needed. Where more detail is needed, the extensive further reading list at the end may be helpful.

The focus is on charitable voluntary organisations in the UK with total incomes in the range £5,000 to £500,000 – but larger and smaller groups will also find the book useful. Much of the content will also be relevant to voluntary organisations without charitable status. But as explained in chapter 1, the impact of the various Charities Acts means many voluntary organisations that do not think of themselves as charities are in fact charitable in law. So the principles of this book apply to nearly all voluntary organisations, other than political organisations and private clubs.

One of the difficulties of charity law arises from the different legal systems in the different countries of the UK. The book starts from the position in England and Wales (now updated in this third edition to allow for the Charities Act 2006 and further changes in 2009) but also seeks to highlight differences in Scotland and in Northern Ireland. Scotland now has an extensive framework for charity accounting as a result of the Charities and Trustee Investment (Scotland) Act 2005, and the Charities Act (Northern Ireland) 2008 at last allows an accounting regime for charities in Northern Ireland.

Legal and similar issues are stated in terms of the position as at 1 June 2010. But a book of this kind can only give an overview of legal issues – there are often more detailed requirements, exceptions and special cases which cannot be covered here. When a charity is in any doubt, it is often wise to take professional advice.

For the second and third edition, I have also taken the opportunity to update many sections to clarify issues that have become particularly important to the sector over the last few years. These include the accounting issues when voluntary organisations get involved in providing public services, the differences between grants and contracts and the whole area of full cost recovery. I have also added some material on partnership arrangements in the sector. The third edition also addresses many legal and threshold changes in the last two years.

This edition also includes developments in the Charities SORP, and more on the accounting framework for different charitable structures: particularly the updated rules for charitable companies as a result of the Companies Act 2006 and the new structure of charitable incorporated organisations.

The central message of the book is that being a charity treasurer or finance officer is an important and worthwhile role. It involves much more than keeping the books: the treasurer or finance officer is a key person in all kinds of strategic decisions and in ensuring the organisation meets the requirements of charity law. Contrary to popular belief, the role does not require massive accounting knowledge, or a brilliant head for figures: simply a commitment to the importance of financial resources, and a willingness to see them used effectively for the purposes of the charity.

Acknowledgements

Over the years I have been enormously privileged to work with several hundred charitable organisations in terms of their accounting and financial arrangements, in many cases helping them to implement procedures to reflect the new charity accounting rules, and in several cases acting as their independent examiner. Others have attended courses I presented, and raised significant questions which have caused me to reflect. Many of the ideas in this book derive from the insights of those organisations, and I would like to dedicate the book to them.

I am also very appreciative of many individuals who have offered advice, listened to my questions and been willing to debate different approaches to charity accounting. This includes key figures in the Charity Commission and OSCR, senior charity accountants, academic colleagues, members of the Council of the Association of Charity Independent Examiners (ACIE) and students on my courses.

I am also most grateful to the Directory of Social Change for inviting me to produce a book on this topic. My wife, Sharon, who is also my partner in Kubernesis, has given a great deal of encouragement to this project and agreed to the inclusion of certain Kubernesis materials.

Nevertheless, I must stress that all opinions expressed are my own (unless another source is mentioned) and any errors remain my responsibility.

Third edition

I would like to express thanks to many people who kindly commented favourably on the first two editions. However, the regulation of charities has changed considerably in the last eight years, with new Charities Acts now on the Statute Book in England and Wales, in Scotland and also in Northern Ireland, so I am grateful to the Directory of Social Change for inviting me to prepare a third edition.

The acknowledgements above continue to apply for this edition, but in addition I would like to acknowledge the contributions of students on my MSc Charity Resource Management course at Sheffield Hallam University, and several further years of work with the ACIE on policy issues, which has greatly deepened my understanding of some of the wider impact of charity accounting.

Gareth G Morgan
York
April 2010

About the author

Gareth Morgan is Professor of Charity Studies at Sheffield Hallam University. He is course leader of the MSc in Charity Resource Management and he leads the University's Centre for Voluntary Sector Research which brings together 13 staff in various faculties with specific interests in the sector. He has published research on various issues of charity regulation and accounting, particularly in relation to small and medium-sized charities, and he contributed proposals for the Bill which became the Charities Act 2006. He has also worked on a range of research projects concerned with voluntary sector infrastructure support including areas such as community accountancy services, funding advice projects and the impact of the Futurebuilders programme.

Outside the university he is also part-time Senior Partner of the York-based charity consultants The Kubernesis Partnership LLP, which supports a wide range of charitable organisations in the areas of accounting, financial management and charity law. He is a Fellow of the Association of Charity Independent Examiners (ACIE) and he served from 1999–2004 as the first general secretary of the Association. He continues work with the ACIE on policy issues.

He is also a member of the Charity Law Association where he has contributed to several working parties, and he is a Certificated Full Member of the Institute of Fundraising and an Academic Fellow of the Association of International Accountants.

He is a trustee of two charities, and over the years has served as treasurer to a number of charitable organisations.

Foreword

Treasurers are as varied as the charities they serve. They can bring a wealth of experience and expertise to the role, or be relative novices. One thing that many of them have in common is that they probably blinked first when jobs were being handed out at the AGM. A second is the subsequent task of persuading their fellow trustees that it is not the treasurer's job to take on sole responsibility for the financial management of their charity.

This book is a gem. All charity treasurers – and anyone else involved in charity finance – should read it through from cover to cover at least once, take a highlighter pen to the margins, turn down the corners of pages, or be conversant with the index, and be ready for when they need to refer to it again.

With his usual thoroughness, Gareth provides both the framework and the detail of what a charity treasurer needs to know, whatever his or her level of expertise. In a time when charity accounting is going through unprecedented change, this is particularly important.

What this book also does, however, is place the role of the treasurer in the context of the wider themes of good governance and the consequent public confidence in charities. For those weary days, therefore, when the missing £1 can't be found or the volunteers don't understand the importance of submitting expense claims on time, here is encouragement to count to ten, take a deep breath and continue the good work.

Fiona Gordon
Director
Association of Charity Independent Examiners

1 Finance in charities and voluntary organisations

Before taking on the role of being a treasurer or finance officer in a charity, you need to understand what is meant by a charity. Charitable status makes a huge difference to the need for accounting and financial management. But many more organisations are charities than people often realise and, as we will see, the term 'charity' actually includes a very large part of the voluntary sector.

Many people think that 'charity' applies only to certain types of organisations with a particular legal form, and which are registered with the Charity Commission: this is quite wrong. There are many possible legal structures for a charity, and there are many organisations which in law are charities, even though historically they were not generally required to be registered: churches are probably the largest such category. Also, the Charity Commission only covers England and Wales; in Scotland the Office of the Scottish Charity Regulator (OSCR) registers charities and there is now also a Charity Commission for Northern Ireland (CCNI). Moreover, many organisations are charitable companies, which means they are subject to both charity and company law.

The principles of being a charity treasurer, and most of the law on charity accounting, apply to almost all charitable organisations.

The third sector, voluntary sector and charity sector

To understand charities, we need to begin with the widest possible view. People often refer to voluntary or not-for-profit (NFP) organisations as the 'third sector'. The government's definition of the third sector is organisations which are neither: (a) established primarily for distribution of profit; nor (b) part of the statutory sector. The third sector is usually seen in contrast to the other two sectors – the commercial sector (business organisations) where profit is the central aim, and the public sector (for example government, local authorities and the health service), which, although NFP, is part of the work of the state. It is best to use the term 'not-for-profit' since many businesses going through hard times are non-profit-making in certain years.

The third sector is often divided into two main categories: voluntary organisations and social enterprises although this can be misleading because a voluntary organisation can undertake social enterprise activities (see below).

Voluntary organisations are established voluntarily to advance aims that are non-statutory and NFP. The term is normally used to describe groups and organisations with some definite constitutional form that are working towards a socially beneficial aim. Some are large national organisations (these almost always have charitable status); others may be small community groups with no paid staff. Voluntary organisations will always have volunteers in governance of the organisation (who may be called trustees or management committee members) and may have volunteers in other roles. Some people prefer to talk of 'voluntary and community organisations' (VCOs), and hence the 'voluntary and community sector' (VCS), but in this book the term 'voluntary organisation' is used to include small community groups, faith-based organisations and, indeed, any organisation which meets these criteria.

Many voluntary organisations are charities (see below) but there are some organisations which, although voluntarily governed and with socially beneficial aims, do not meet the precise requirements of charitable status. An example would be a group set up to raise funds purely to support one person or family.

Social enterprises, on the other hand, if separately constituted, are trading organisations where profit may be an explicit aim, even though the purpose of the trade is for the benefit of the community. They do not have to be voluntarily governed – they can have paid board members if resources allow. Some are structured as cooperatives, where the members share in the profits. Since 2005, many social enterprises have been established using the new legal structure of a community interest company (CIC). CICs are subject to an 'asset lock' – this allows outside investors to receive a modest return if required but most of the profits must be retained for the social aims of the organisation. However, cooperatives and CICs are *not* charities, and so they are not directly considered in this book.

But the term 'social enterprise' can get confused, because charities often undertake trading activities, and many describe these activities as 'social enterprise'. In particular, some kinds of government support for social enterprise can include trading activities undertaken by charities. Also, as mentioned in chapter 11, some larger charities may have a subsidiary company that undertakes non-charitable trading activities (with the aim of making a profit for the charity), which are often classed as 'social enterprises'. So in this book we use the term 'charity trading' to describe trading activities undertaken directly by an organisation with charitable status, as the term 'social enterprise' can include both charitable and non-charitable trading.

As well as voluntary organisations and social enterprises, the third sector can also be considered to include other kinds of NFP organisations, for example trade unions, political parties, trade associations and private members clubs, but none of these can be charities.

The financial management of NFP organisations is obviously quite different from profit-making organisations: the central aims are usually concerned with providing services or making a positive difference to the world. Making a profit is never the main aim of the third sector, and certainly NFP organisations must be non-profit-distributing – that is, if they do make a profit or surplus one year, it is retained to support the work of the organisation in future years, not distributed to owners or shareholders.

To most people the word 'profit' implies profits being taken out, so it is best to avoid this term in the NFP sector: occasionally you may want to talk about the profit on a certain activity, but you cannot meaningfully talk about the profit of a charity as a whole. If a charity's income exceeds its expenditure in a given year, we say it has made a 'surplus' (or a 'deficit' if the expenditure was more than the income). Of course the income and expenditure will never be exactly equal, and in most NFP organisations a small surplus one year will be balanced by a small deficit another year. Sometimes surpluses are needed for a few years to build up sufficient reserves (see chapter 4), but it can never be right for a charity to be making surpluses indefinitely, as it would mean substantial amounts of income were not being spent on the charity's objects. This is a big contrast to the commercial sector, where a profit is normally sought every year.

There are some similarities between the public sector and the third sector in terms of bidding for resources and managing budgets; the fundamental difference is that public sector organisations are under government direction (national or local), whereas organisations in the voluntary sector are regarded as independent and can set their own directions and priorities.

This does not mean that voluntary organisations are totally free of government control. They must obviously obey the laws of the land (including a number of specific issues of charity law and general issues such as employment and health and safety law) and many voluntary organisations get at least part of their income from the government, for example through grants or gift aid tax refunds on donations (see chapter 12). But at the end of the day, a third sector organisation is primarily accountable to its own stakeholders, for example its members, trustees and beneficiaries.

A relationship of trust

This independence also creates a special relationship with funders and donors: a relationship of trust. Much income to charities (and to many other voluntary organisations) relies on money that is *given* to the organisation. Few people would make donations to commercial businesses or to the public sector, but people routinely give to charities and to other NFP organisations without seeking anything in return other than an expectation that their gifts will be used to advance the organisation's aims.

This does not just apply to personal donations; most grants, whether from the public sector or from other charities, are *given* to a charity. Grants and donations may be subject to specific conditions on the use of the money – this gives rise to restricted funds (see chapter 3) – but ultimately the relationship with the funder or donor is one in which money is given and the charity is entrusted with using it properly.

This is in complete contrast to commercial organisations, where most of the income is from sales, in which the relationship is contractual (for example 'We will let you have this tin of paint if you pay us £5.50'). Charities can also have contractual income (trading income – see chapter 11), and for some charities this can be the main form of income, but for many charities money that is given is their main source of funds.

This relationship of trust is central to understanding voluntary sector finance, and is also the reason why much charity law is part of trust law. For this reason, those who have the day to day control of a charity (for example a management committee, church council or directors of a charitable company) are called 'trustees': they are entrusted with funds given by others to advance the charity's aims. However, the trust relationship can also apply elsewhere in the sector, for example with gifts to political organisations. Any grant or donation to a voluntary organisation implies some kind of trust relationship.

Trustees who fail to respect such relationships are guilty of a breach of trust, a serious matter that can result in court action. In extreme cases, a trustee who recklessly commits a breach of trust might have to reimburse the charity personally for money that was wrongly used.

In some NFP organisations it is common for board members to be paid – for example, in the public sector many people serving on trust boards are entitled to allowances or salaries, and this can also apply to non-charitable social enterprises. But a central issue of charity law is that charity trustees must be unpaid: they can, naturally, be reimbursed expenses, but the role of being a charity trustee is essentially voluntary. This clearly includes the treasurer, since a charity treasurer is normally a key trustee (except in rare cases where someone takes on the treasurership without having the right to vote at trustees' meetings).

There are some exceptions to this rule. A few charities have special governing instruments allowing certain trustees to be paid and, subject to very strict criteria, the Charities Act 2006 allows a charity to pay a trustee for specific services outside their role as a trustee. In other one-off cases a charity can apply for individual approval from the Charity Commission for a transaction with a trustee. But these are relatively rare, and excluding these cases, paying anything to a trustee other than reimbursement of expenses is a clear breach of trust. As shown in figure 7.4 on pages 100–101, to help safeguard against abuses, any payments to trustees must normally be shown separately in the charity's published accounts.

The principle of unpaid governance is at the heart of the voluntary sector, and even non-charitable voluntary organisations will find it hard to get grants if their committee members are paid. Some people question the term 'voluntary sector', pointing out that many charities nowadays do much of their work through paid staff, with limited use of volunteers. But all voluntary organisations rely on volunteers at the trustee level.

(For more information on trusteeship, see the *Charity Trustee's Handbook*, also in this series.)

What is a charity?

For any organisation to be a charity, it must clearly be a voluntary organisation, with a group of people – the trustees – responsible on an unpaid basis for deciding on the use of the funds (subject to any conditions imposed by donors).

But not all voluntary organisations are charities. However, the test of charitable status does not depend on a certain structure nor on registration with the Charity Commission or OSCR or the CCNI. Rather it depends on two key tests.

- The organisation must have exclusively charitable objects. This principle goes back to a 1601 statute of Elizabeth I, but from 2008 a new list of charitable purposes defined by the Charities Act 2006 takes effect. To be charitable, the objects of the organisation must fit entirely into one or more of following:
  - (a) the prevention and relief of poverty;
  - (b) the advancement of education;
  - (c) the advancement of religion;
  - (d) the advancement of health or the saving of lives;
  - (e) the advancement of citizenship or community development (this includes rural or urban regeneration, the promotion of civic responsibility, volunteering, the voluntary sector or the effectiveness and efficiency of charities in general);
  - (f) the advancement of arts, heritage, culture or science;
  - (g) the advancement of amateur sport;
  - (h) the advancement of human rights, conflict resolution or reconciliation or the promotion of religious or racial harmony or equality or diversity;
  - (i) the advancement of environmental protection or improvement;
  - (j) the relief of those in need by reason of youth, age, ill-health, disability, financial hardship or other disadvantage;
  - (k) the advancement of animal welfare;
  - (l) the promotion of the efficiency of the armed forces or emergency services;
  - (m) any other purpose which may reasonably be regarded as analogous to the above (including purposes under existing charity law).

- The organisation must exist for public benefit. In other words, it must seek to benefit a wide range of people (and there must be no private benefit; for example, except in very exceptional cases, the trustees must be unpaid): the Charity Commission has issued guidance on this which trustees are required to consider.

These charitable purposes apply to England and Wales (although the list above has been slightly paraphrased from the Act). However, there are some slight differences in Scotland (with slightly tighter rules on public benefit) and further slight differences in Northern Ireland. If a charity is to operate throughout the UK, the objects need to be worded in order to meet the requirements of all three systems of charity law.

It is clear that a very wide range of voluntary organisations seeking to do work that most people would regard as worthwhile can fit into one or more of these categories if they word their governing document appropriately.

In England and Wales, the Charity Commission decides whether a particular organisation meets the criteria for charitable status (although in case of disagreement it is possible to appeal to the Charity Tribunal and ultimately to the courts). In Scotland, decisions are made by OSCR. In Northern Ireland, until recently charities were recognised purely under tax law by HM Revenue & Customs (HMRC), but that role is now transferring to the CCNI.

It follows that the governing document of the charity (its constitution, articles of association, trust deed or rules – see *Legal forms*, page 8) is vital in determining charitable status. In particular, the objects of the organisation (as stated in the governing document) and the range of beneficiaries are central to this decision. In theory it is possible to have a charity without a written constitution – occasionally people make the mistake of launching major appeals without any written documents. In such cases the charitable status of the funds raised would depend on witnesses testifying to what had been said at the time. But in the long term it is very hard to raise funds without a formal structure.

In practice, the main voluntary organisations excluded from charitable status tend to be:

- those whose aims are deemed in law to be primarily political, for example, campaigning organisations whose main aim is to achieve a change in the law;
- those not offering sufficient public benefit, for example a tenants' group working purely with the tenants in a given block of flats or a club whose facilities are only available to its members (unless the membership rules make it easy for anyone to join).

Unless your organisation is clearly excluded from charitable status, it is safest to work on the assumption (at least for accounting purposes) that it is a charity, until proven otherwise. This means producing accounts to comply with charity law and, in England and Wales, the trustees must apply for the charity to be registered unless it is clearly excepted or exempt (see *Charitable status*, page 12).

Furthermore, you will not qualify for charity tax concessions unless your charitable status is clearly established. There is no 'half-way house' on this issue – a non-charitable voluntary organisation is treated as a business for tax purposes. If its only income is from grants and donations it is unlikely to incur tax except on investment income, but if it has any trading activities that make a profit (such as journal subscriptions or selling tickets for an event) the committee must make a corporation tax return to HMRC and must expect to pay tax. There are certain concessions in relation to 'mutual trading', but if you run a voluntary organisation that plans to rely on this, you should certainly seek advice from an accountant with experience in the tax affairs of clubs and associations.

As a charity treasurer or finance officer, you do not need to be an expert on charitable status, but you do need to understand the basic framework for your organisation's status, and you must certainly be aware of its charitable objects as stated in the governing document. (See *Further reading* for sources of further information.)

Legal forms

Charities can have one of a number of legal structures; once you have a copy of your governing document it should be clear which structure applies. Table 1.1 shows most of the main structures.

Until recently the vast majority of new charities were established using one of the first three structures, but the charitable incorporated organisation (CIO) form introduced by the Charities Act 2006 is expected to become very popular – see below. However, some charities have other structures not shown in this table – particularly with long-established organisations.

To form a new charity, a charitable trust is the simplest structure: all that is needed is for someone to make an initial donation (the 'settlor') and by means of a trust deed the objects are defined and initial trustees appointed. Most grant-making charities use this structure.

For a more democratic structure, with members electing a committee to act as trustees, the charitable association is the easiest model. Essentially, a group of people with common interests agree to associate themselves together, and agree to a constitution or set of rules that determines the criteria for membership and the procedures for electing the committee. A wide range of local community-based charities and service-providing organisations use this structure. But it is vital to keep proper records, to distinguish between ordinary members of the association (who have the right to vote at the annual general meeting – AGM) and members of the committee (who have day to day control of funds and are thus the trustees of the charity).

Table 1.1   Legal structures

Legal form	Governing document	Usual internal term for trustees
Charitable trust	Trust deed (or a will, or a Scheme created by the Charity Commission)	Trustees
Charitable association	Constitution	Committee
Charitable company (company limited by guarantee – CLG)	Articles of association	Directors or board members
Charitable incorporated organisation (CIO)	Constitution	Trustees
Community benefit society (CBS or bencom – industrial and provident society established for the benefit of the community)	Rules	Committee
Charities established by Royal Charter (for example Scouts/Guides and certain professional bodies)	Charter	Council
Charities established by Act of Parliament (for example most Church of England bodies)	Act of Parliament (or regulations made under the Act)	Various terms

A charitable company is created by establishing a NFP company (a company limited by guarantee – CLG) under company law and then applying for the company to be registered as a charity. A company has the advantage of being a legally separate 'incorporated' entity: this means, for example, that if the charity needs to purchase freehold property it can be registered in the name of the charity, rather than in the names of individual trustees. Also, if the charity enters into a contract that goes wrong, and the charity finds itself being sued, the rules of limited liability apply, i.e. the charity's own resources could be lost in a court action, but the trustees could not be sued personally for breach of contract. In unincorporated charities, such as trusts and associations, if something goes wrong, the trustees could, in theory, be personally liable.

However, the protections of limited liability apply only to charitable companies if the directors/trustees have complied with all the requirements of company law. This gives a vast range of legal responsibilities over and above the requirements of charity law so, for example, unless you know what is meant in company law by 'wrongful trading' and how to avoid it, limited liability is of little help. Also, limited liability is only relevant in contract law; if, for example, you misuse restricted funds (see chapter 3), this is a breach of trust. Further, many risks can be mitigated in all types of charities by appropriate insurance: for example, charities giving advice certainly need professional indemnity insurance. Allowing the whole charity to collapse because of one disgruntled person taking legal action is hardly a good strategy in the first place: limited liability might protect the trustees, but staff would lose their jobs and beneficiaries would lose out. Finally, it has to be said that it is very rare for charity trustees acting in good faith to find themselves facing legal action; the bad publicity that would arise from suing a group of volunteers would put most people off.

However, a CIO overcomes most of the disadvantages of the first three forms. A CIO is governed purely by charity law and is created simply by being registered with the Charity Commission but it is an incorporated body with limited liability – thus giving most of the benefits of the charitable company without all the additional requirements of company law. The first CIOs are expected to be registered from early 2011. In Scotland, the legislation allows for a similar structure, registered by OSCR, known as a Scottish charitable incorporated organisation (SCIO) and CIOs will be possible in Northern Ireland through registration with CCNI.

In due course it is likely that most new charities will adopt the CIO form and many existing charities may choose to convert to CIOs. However, there is no requirement to convert – many charities use the existing structures and these are likely to continue for some time.

Box 1.2   Key abbreviations for NFP structures

Take care with the abbreviations:

CIO   Charitable incorporated organisation – a CIO is *always* a charity.

CIC   Community interest company (social enterprise) – a CIC is *never* a charity.

CLG   Company limited by guarantee. A CLG *may* be a charity. Most CLGs are NFP organisations but they do not have to be charities. A CLG that is a charity is described as a *charitable company*.

CBS   Community benefit society (an industrial and provident society with community aims) – also known as a 'bencom'. A CBS is *usually* a charity, but this is not essential.

As a treasurer or finance officer, you need to be clear about the structure for which you are accounting. If your organisation is a charitable company, your accounting procedures must comply with company law as well as charity law; a number of differences are highlighted in the following chapters. But a CIO is *not* a company and the normal accounting rules apply for charities that are not companies.

Incorporation of existing charities

Sometimes a charity which is established as a charitable trust or association wishes to convert to an incorporated body – i.e. to become a charitable company or a CIO. This is sometimes described loosely as 'incorporating the charity' but in law an unincorporated body cannot take on a new legal form. In practice, what happens is that a *new* charity is formed (a charitable company or a CIO) and then the *old* charity is wound up and all the assets transferred to the new organisation. This has important accounting implications: the old and new charities are separate organisations, with separate charity registration numbers, and in the year of the change two separate sets of published accounts are needed (unless the old organisation can be wound up exactly on the last day of its accounting year). A treasurer handling such a conversion thus needs to keep completely separate books for the old and new organisations.

Subsidiary groups

Another vital issue on the legal structure, which is often overlooked, is to be clear on the boundaries of your organisation: as treasurer, you need some control over *all* the finances of the charity that are in any way managed by your trustees. If you have several funds or projects, your accounts must reflect them all. Furthermore, many charities have groups that run their own finances, but which see themselves as part of the main charity. For example, a community association may run an older people's support group, and may have an arts and drama club meeting on its premises. As treasurer, you must be clear whether each such group is:

- legally part of your charity – if so, its work is under the control of the charity's trustees, and its finances must be included in the published accounts of the charity; or
- an independent organisation simply using your premises – if so, it must not attempt to use your charity registration number, and if its income is more than £5,000 (England and Wales) it will normally need to be registered as a charity in its own right.

This is also important when charities hand out funds to local groups. If you give money to independent groups, there must be a clear point when the grant ceases to be in the funds of your charity and control passes to the separate group. But if the main charity passes money to a group which is still legally part of that charity, your accounts will simply show a transfer between funds: no money has gone out of the charity as a whole.

A few charities also have separately constituted subsidiary organisations that are under their direct control, for example trading subsidiary companies (see chapter 11). In this case, the subsidiary has to prepare its own accounts, but they may then need to be included ('consolidated') into the accounts of the main charity. If this applies you will need help from an accountant or independent examiner with experience of group accounts.

Charitable status

As explained above, many different organisations can be charities, and not all charities are registered. There are currently five forms of charitable status recognised in the UK.

- *Exempt charities* (England and Wales) – a small number of bodies listed in Schedule 2 of the Charities Act 1993. They are mainly large national bodies whose charitable activities are regulated by a body other than the Charity Commission (for example universities and registered social landlords). Much of the Charities Act 1993 does not apply to exempt charities, but the Charities Statement of Recommended Practice (SORP) (see chapter 2) is still the normal basis for presenting the accounts, unless a more specialised SORP applies.

- *Excepted charities* (England and Wales) – these are excepted from registration under sections 3 and 3A of the Charities Act 1993 (as amended by the Charities Act 2006) but they are still subject to other aspects of the Act, including the accounting rules. For example, charities whose annual income is £5,000 or less are excepted from registration. As a result of the 2006 Act, the category of excepted charities will be greatly reduced and the majority of charities that were previously excepted (for example, places of worship, Scout and Guide groups and armed forces charities) will be required to register as charities in the normal way. However, this is being introduced gradually: at present only the formerly excepted charities with more than £100,000 income are required to register, then gradually over the years this limit will be reduced. This will also apply to formerly exempt charities such as community benefit societies.

- *Registered charities* – all other charities in England and Wales must be registered by the Charity Commission, and are given a 'registered charity number'. This status must appear on many documents, including cheques, invoices, receipts and bills.

- *Scottish charities* – these are registered by the OSCR and are given a Scottish charity number, beginning with 'SC'. It should be noted that charity registration is now compulsory in Scotland – there is no £5,000 lower limit as in England and Wales. If a Scottish organisation chooses not to register, it is illegal for it to call itself a charity on any literature or documents.

- *Northern Irish charities* – until recently all decisions on charitable status in Northern Ireland were made by HMRC, but a register of charities for Northern Ireland took effect from 2010 and charity registrations in Northern Ireland will soon involve application to CCNI. For organisations established in Northern Ireland there is no lower limit for charity registration.

So it is vital to appreciate that charitable status is not an optional 'badge'. Even in England and Wales, it is compulsory under the Charities Act 1993 for the trustees of a charitable organisation to apply for registration unless it is clearly exempted or excepted (and they are committing a breach of duty if they fail to do so). It follows that, once all the legislation is fully in force, any voluntary organisation in the UK will need to apply for charitable recognition unless:

(a) its aims are clearly non-charitable; or
(b) it clearly would not meet the test of public benefit; or
(c) it operates purely in England and Wales and has income of £5,000 or less.

In the case of a CIO, the organisation only comes into being once it is registered with the Charity Commission (or CCNI, or OSCR in the case of an SCIO). So a CIO is a registered charity from the outset. In this respect, CIOs are different from all the other legal forms – in other cases there is always a period between the organisation being formed and its formal recognition as a charity.

In the case of a charitable company, the registration as a CLG (with Companies House) and charity registration (with the Charity Commission or OSCR or CCNI) are completely separate; the charity must report each year to both regulators.

UK-wide issues

All five forms of charitable status mean that the organisation is a charity for the purpose of the law. Moreover, in terms of tax law, all UK charities have the same tax concessions (tax law is determined UK-wide, it is not devolved to the different jurisdictions of the UK). However, there are some possible complications: charitable status for tax purposes is determined by the English definition of 'charity' and hence it is possible in theory that a Scottish charity could be registered with OSCR but fall outside the tax definition of a charity. From 2010 there is also a tax law requirement for charities to be managed by 'fit and proper persons'. But the definitions are so close (and, if anything, the Scottish and Northern Irish definitions are slightly tighter than that in England and Wales) that, in practice, there is little risk of a well run charity anywhere in the UK failing the tax definition of a 'charity'.

If a charity's work spreads across several countries of the UK, its location for charity law is normally determined by the wording of its governing document, or if this is not specific, by the location of the majority of the trustees.

However, an important new development in recent years is that many UK-wide charities are now subject to *dual regulation*. If a charity established under the law of England and Wales has regular activities in Scotland then, under the Charities and Trustee Investment (Scotland) Act 2005, it will need to be registered with OSCR *as well* as being registered with the Charity Commission. If this applies, the charity must account to OSCR as well as to the Charity Commission. Its accounts must then comply with the Scottish charity accounting rules, as well as the rules for England and Wales. In most respects the Scottish rules are tighter, so, *if you are a treasurer or finance officer of a dual-registered charity, in general you should follow the guidance for Scottish charities throughout this book, even if only a small part of the charity's work is in Scotland.*

If a charity simply fundraises in Scotland (for example, if you have members or supporters in Scotland, but do not have any regular use of premises in Scotland) registration with OSCR is not required, but all your literature must make clear the country where you are established. So, for example, if you are making use of this rule, rather than just putting 'Registered charity number xxxxxx' on your literature, take care to put 'Registered charity in England and Wales number xxxxxx'.

Note that there is no converse requirement: charities established under Scottish law and registered with OSCR do not have to register with the Charity Commission in order to operate in England or Wales.

The rules are slightly lighter in Northern Ireland – an external charity operating in NI does not have to be registered on the main CCNI register but instead on a simpler register – the so-called 'section 167 register', though this will not start until at least 2011/12. But eventually a UK-wide charity formed under English law will need to be registered with the Charity Commission, and with OSCR and on the section 167 register with the CCNI – and will have to make returns to all three regulators.

The Charity Commission, OSCR and CCNI

In England and Wales, much of the regulation of charities, and many of the requirements for charity accounting – such as the Directions to independent examiners – are handled through the Charity Commission. The Commission has various powers defined by the Charities Act 1993, which were increased by the Charities Act 2006. It is a government department, but independent of direct day to day government control. All registered charities have to complete an annual form for the Commission, and the Commission has extensive powers to intervene to protect charitable funds where abuse appears to be taking place. OSCR has many similar powers in Scotland, and likewise the CCNI in Northern Ireland.

Some charity treasurers mistakenly feel their task is largely about keeping the Charity Commission happy. This is misleading – the Commission's requirements are only one small part of a treasurer's role – but as a charity treasurer, you will need to ensure that your accounts are sent to the Commission each year (and/or to OSCR/CCNI) and you will probably be responsible for completing much of the annual return. However, you will also find the regulators are a helpful source of information and guidance, particularly in terms of their websites and publications – see *Further reading* for more details.

If you are a treasurer of an excepted charity in England and Wales – which currently includes most places of worship under £100,000 income – you do not normally have to send accounts to the Charity Commission every year. But your charity is still subject to the Charities Act accounting provisions and almost all the Commission's guidance materials are just as relevant as for registered charities. The Charity Commission has the same powers to take action if it believes that charitable funds are at risk.

2 Accounts at different levels: the legal requirements

When someone asks to look at your accounts, this can have a number of meanings. The term 'accounts' can cover everything from the detailed books and records to the final published accounts, and anything in-between.

Levels of detail

For most charities, accounts will work at three levels of detail – see table 2.1.

Table 2.1 Accounting levels

Concept	Official term
THE BOOKS Record of all transactions Must show the financial position of the charity at any time and be kept for six years. Must be seen by the charity's auditor or independent examiner – otherwise for internal use only.	**Accounting records**
INTERIM REPORTS Typically reports for trustees or key members of staff to monitor progress and take financial decisions. Will not usually show individual transactions, but generally summarise figures for a period of less than a year. May show actuals against budgets and possibly future projections. For internal use only.	**Management accounts**
PUBLISHED YEAR END ACCOUNTS Show financial position of whole charity	**Financial statements** or **annual accounts** or just **the accounts**

All charities, no matter how small, must produce published accounts, which must be approved by the trustees. Includes report by auditor or independent examiner (unless under £25,000 income in England and Wales). The annual accounts should always be circulated with the annual report. They are a public document – anyone can ask for a copy.

The accounts start with the basic books of the charity, where every transaction – every receipt, payment or other entry – is recorded individually. The formal term for these is your *accounting records*. As a treasurer or finance officer, you must ensure books are kept up to date with all the relevant entries – chapter 5 explores ways of handling the bookkeeping. The books are the starting point for all other financial analysis.

This is a fundamental difference between charity accounting and personal accounting. With your personal household accounts you can, if you choose, just look at your bank balance and count the cash in your purse or wallet without ever recording the actual income and expenditure. In fact, even some self-employed business people manage to work with minimal records (although this can make it hard to justify profit figures to HM Revenue & Customs – HMRC). But in a charity, the trustees are handling other people's money, and you have both a legal and a moral obligation to keep detailed records of the income as it comes in, and exactly how it is spent.

However, if you have more than about 20 or 30 transactions, it is difficult for anyone to get an idea of how the charity is doing just by looking at the books. You need some way of summarising the records into a form that will be meaningful for taking decisions. Such internal summaries of the books are called *management accounts*. Normally they will show the total income under headings such as 'donations, sales, bank interest', and the expenditure under headings such as 'salaries, premises, printing' and so on, rather than listing every transaction. If you have several funds or projects (see chapter 3) the management accounts will also be broken down by fund. Where budgets have been agreed, management accounts are often presented showing actual figures compared with budgets (see chapter 9).

One of the important tasks of the treasurer or finance officer is to produce regular management accounts for the trustees. In a small charity this may be just a one-page summary, but regular meaningful financial information is essential for decision making.

The third form of accounts is the final year end published accounts – the *annual accounts* – see chapter 7. One of the conditions of charitable status is that your organisation must, once a year, make available a full set of accounts reporting the income and expenditure for the year, the balances at year end, and the different funds involved. The annual accounts must always be accompanied by the *trustees' annual report* (see chapter 7) – so the full document is usually called the 'annual report and accounts'.

If your organisation is a registered charity in England and Wales then (except for those with an income of £25,000 or less) the annual report and accounts must be sent to the Charity Commission. Likewise, if the charity is registered in Scotland the accounts must be sent to the Office of the Scottish Charity Regulator (OSCR) and similarly with the CCNI in Northern Ireland. Charitable companies must *also* file an annual report and accounts and annual return at Companies House (for which there is a fee). But, more importantly, copies of the annual report and accounts must be made available to *anyone* on request. (You can make a small charge to cover copying and postage if necessary, although in practice many charities wish to be as open as possible and publish their annual report and accounts on their website. But even if you do not do this, for charities registered with the Charity Commission over £25,000 income, accounts are available from the Commission's website – what you submit is scanned in for publication or you can file the accounts electronically as a PDF.) Different formats apply to different sizes of charity, but even a tiny charity with only £100 per year income must still produce published accounts – there is no such thing as a secret charity, whatever its size.

The time limit for filing accounts is generally nine months after year end (this is the time limit for charities registered with OSCR and for charitable companies). For a charity with a 31 March year end, and allowing for Christmas holidays, this means that in practice you need to submit your accounts no later than about 15 December. However, charities registered *only* with the Charity Commission can take up to 10 months. But an organised charity should be able to submit accounts well before these deadlines: funders will often check the Charity Commission website, and delays in filing accounts can easily affect future support.

The books and management accounts will normally be the responsibility of the treasurer and any staff with a finance role. As treasurer or finance officer, you may have the task of *drafting* the final accounts, but *approving* the published accounts is one of the key actions of the trustees as a whole in taking responsibility for the affairs of the charity.

The legal framework and the SORP

Charity accounts are governed extensively by law, as summarised in table 2.2. In most respects, the rules on charity accounting are more extensive than those for commercial accounts: this is because charities are entrusted with other people's money and have a duty to use those funds for public benefit. Charity accounting requirements have changed enormously since the early 1990s, and have also changed further in each year 2005–2009; even many professional accountants, if they are not charity specialists, may be unaware of the full implications.

Table 2.2   The basis of the law on charity accounting

England and Wales
- Charities Act 1993 (Part VI) [as amended by Charities Act 2006]
- Charities (Accounts and Reports) Regulations 2008
- Charities SORP (see below)
- Charity Commission Directions and Guidance (in some areas these have the force of law, especially the Directions to Independent Examiners)

Scotland
- Charities and Trustee Investment (Scotland) Act 2005
- Charities Accounts (Scotland) Regulations 2006
- Charities SORP (see below)
- Guidance from OSCR may also be helpful (but it does not have the force of law)

Northern Ireland
- Charities Act (Northern Ireland) 2008
- Northern Ireland charity accounting regulations (when finalised)
- Charities SORP (see below)
- CCNI Directions and Guidance

The Charities SORP
- Statement of Recommended Practice on Accounting and Reporting by Charities
- Published by the Charity Commission with approval by the Accounting Standards Board (the latest version is SORP 2005 although updates may be made from time to time). The SORP applies throughout the UK and to all charities, including charitable companies.

(See *Further reading* for sources of these documents.)

In England and Wales, most current charity law comes from the Charities Act 1993 (as amended) which, either directly or by Regulations, gives considerable detail on what a charity must do in terms of accounting. In Scotland, the 2005 Act includes a general power to make rules on charity accounting, but all the specifics are in the Charities Accounts (Scotland) Regulations 2006. In Northern Ireland the 2008 Act has many similarities to England with some requirements in the Act itself and other issues left to Regulations, though final regulations implementing the accounting framework are not expected until autumn 2011.

For charitable companies, the legal framework for accounts depends on the Companies Act 2006, rather than the legislation shown in table 2.2, but company accounts must follow relevant accounting standards and the Charities SORP is an essential standard where the company is a charity.

In all parts of the UK, a major addition to the regulations comes from the *Statement of Recommended Practice on Accounting and Reporting by Charities*, usually abbreviated to the 'Charities SORP' or just 'SORP' – often with the relevant year to refer to the latest version, e.g. 'SORP 2005'. In practice, people often talk about the whole regime as the SORP, as in the question 'Are your accounts SORP-compliant?'.

Firstly, you might think that, as the title includes the word 'recommended', you can ignore the SORP if you wish, but in fact it is compulsory in many respects. Any accounts designed to give a 'true and fair view' should comply with relevant accounting standards. (For example, with charitable companies, the 'true and fair view' is a requirement of the Companies Acts, and with other charities it is a requirement of the accounting regulations except for smaller charities producing receipts and payments accounts – see *Accruals or receipts and payments?*, page 27) Secondly, in England and Wales, the Charity Commission has stated that it 'expects the accounts of charities and their accounting practices to comply fully with the SORP' and may well use its powers to institute inquiries if they do not. Thirdly, the Regulations, both in England and Wales and in Scotland, are drafted with extensive references to the SORP so, in practice, a large proportion of the SORP is actually made into law. Furthermore, for charities following SORP, the Regulations require that any departures from the SORP must be disclosed by specific notes to the accounts. Finally, most funders nowadays expect SORP-compliant accounts, at least for charities over £250,000 income, and sometimes below this.

So, except for small charities just using receipts and payments accounts, you ignore the SORP at your peril – and in fact, even for receipts and payments, some points in the SORP can still be very helpful.

Thus, in each regime the rules are based on a combination of primary legislation (Acts of Parliament), secondary legislation (regulations issued as statutory instruments) and other standards such as the SORP. But although charity treasurers need an overview of the rules, this book is not attempting to cover the full detail (for more information see *Further reading*).

In some charities there may be additional rules imposed by parent bodies. For example, many national charities with independent local branches require certain information to be shown in the branch accounts as a condition of belonging to the national body or to comply with other legislation, for example the Church Accounting Regulations in the Church of England. But such rules are always additional to the main regime; they cannot override the SORP or relax rules required by law.

What does the law require?

Referring back to the three levels of accounts, in relation to the *books*, the law requires that all charities must keep proper accounting records 'sufficient to disclose, with reasonable accuracy, the financial position of the charity' at any time, including records of their receipts, payments, assets and liabilities. They must also be sufficient to allow the production of proper accounts at year end.

It follows that what is sometimes called 'shoebox accounting', where the treasurer or bookkeeper throws everything in a box and hopes someone else will sort it out at year end, is not only unwise, it is actually illegal. With a shoebox approach there will be many times when the financial position cannot be ascertained.

The law also requires that the records must be kept for six years from the end of the year concerned. If there are changes of treasurer, be sure that the last six years' books and papers are passed on and not destroyed. Also remember that the full records include the bills and vouchers – not just the entries in the books.

However, the law does not prescribe how the books are to be kept. You are free to use any method of bookkeeping, manual or computerised, that will enable the charity to comply with the overall requirements. With computer systems, ensure you have full printouts at year end. Although large organisations sometimes dispense with paper records, for a small charity it is risky to rely on six-year-old computer backups, given the rate of change of hardware and software.

Remember, too, that the full accounting records may be divided between several sets of books or computer systems. If you have staff, your payroll records are part of the books of the charity. If you have people giving individual donations – for example under a gift aid scheme (see chapter 12) – it is unlikely that your main books will show every separate gift, particularly where donors are giving weekly or monthly, so your fundraising records must also be retained. (The need for donor confidentiality does not replace the need for proper records.)

At the second level, the *management accounts*, there are no specific legal requirements. The trustees have a duty to manage the charity properly and, except in a tiny organisation, this will mean monitoring the finances more than once a year, so some kind of interim financial reports are essential (see chapter 9). However, it is for the trustees of each charity to decide what is appropriate.

Most of the law on charity accounting relates to the final level, the published *annual accounts* – references in law to the 'accounts' of a charity mean the published year end accounts. Much of the Regulations and SORP are concerned with the final accounts; chapter 7 outlines some of the steps involved. However, the rules sensibly recognise that a small local charity cannot be expected to produce the same sort of annual accounts as a large national organisation, so the regime has a series of thresholds.

The thresholds

Much of the charity accounting regime is determined by the total income of the charity. For smaller charities, the regime is not particularly onerous; as a charity grows in income, the rules become more demanding. But it is vital to appreciate that all charities, no matter how small, are affected by some rules: occasionally one hears people saying 'I don't need to bother about the Charities Act because our income is under £100,000' – unfortunately this is a serious misunderstanding.

Table 2.3 shows the main accounting requirements at present for charities in England and Wales. Note that there are different rules for charities with assets of more than £3.26 million – though smaller charities are unlikely to be affected by this unless you have a very valuable building or a large investment portfolio. Table 2.4 gives the details for charities registered in Scotland, and table 2.5 shows the rules for Northern Ireland. Note that in each case charitable companies have an additional requirement: they cannot use receipts and payments accounts even if the income is very small. But remember that charitable incorporated organisations (CIOs) and Scottish charitable incorporated organisations (SCIOs) (see *Legal forms*, page 8) are *not* companies, so the rules for non-company charities apply. (Note that if a charity is dual-registered – with the Charity Commission and with OSCR – the Scottish rules are generally stricter so these should be followed even if the charity is based in England or Wales. However, external charities operating in Northern Ireland do not face additional rules on the charity's overall accounts – see *UK-wide issues* page 14).

Table 2.3 Minimum accounting requirements for charities subject to the law of England and Wales

Income of charity	Minimum requirements for charities with not more than £3.26 million assets	Minimum requirements where charity has more than £3.26 million assets
All charities	• Must keep proper accounting records (retained for six years). • Must produce an annual report and accounts: the accounts can be on a receipts and payments basis (*except for charitable companies*, which must use the accruals basis and SORP format whatever the level of income). • Must provide accounts to the Charity Commission if requested and to members of the public on request.	
> £5,000	• Must apply to become a registered charity (unless exempt or excepted). • If registered, must complete the Charity Commission annual database update.	
> £25,000	• Accounts must be independently examined (see chapter 8). • Annual report and accounts must be sent to Charity Commission and must complete Charity Commission annual return (for CIOs this applies even for those under £25,000).	
> £250,000	• Full accruals accounting required. • Presentation of accounts must comply with regulations – with statement of financial activities (SOFA), balance sheet and notes (SORP format) – but simplified SOFA headings are permitted. • Independent examiner must be professionally qualified.	• Full accruals accounting required. • Presentation of accounts must comply with regulations – with SOFA, balance sheet and notes (SORP format) – full SORP compliance required including use of 'functional headings' on the SOFA. • Full audit required.
> £500,000	• Full SORP compliance required, including use of 'functional headings' on the SOFA. • Full audit required.	
> £6.5 million	• Accounts must include cashflow statement.	

See the text for explanation of terms used in this table

Table 2.4   Minimum accounting requirements for charities registered in Scotland

Income of charity	Minimum requirements for charities with not more than £2.8 million* assets	Minimum requirements where charity has over £2.8 million* assets
All charities	<ul><li>Must apply to OSCR to be registered if making any claim to charitable status in Scotland.</li><li>Must keep proper accounting records (retained for six years).</li><li>Must produce an annual report and accounts: the accounts can be on a receipts and payments (R&P) basis, but the detailed Scottish regulations for R&P accounts must be followed (*except for charitable companies* which must use the accruals basis and SORP format whatever the level of income).</li><li>Accounts must be independently examined (see chapter 8).</li><li>Must submit accounts to OSCR and to members of the public on request.</li></ul>	
£100,000+*	<ul><li>Full accruals accounting required.</li><li>Presentation of accounts must comply with Regulations – with SOFA, balance sheet and notes (SORP format) – but simplified SOFA headings are permitted.</li><li>Independent examiner must be professionally qualified (this also applies to charities below £100,000 income if the accounts are on an accruals basis).</li></ul>	<ul><li>Full accruals accounting required.</li><li>Presentation of accounts must comply with Regulations – with SOFA, balance sheet and notes (SORP format).</li><li>Full audit required.</li><li>Full SORP compliance required including use of 'functional headings' on the SOFA.</li></ul>
£500,000+	<ul><li>Full audit required.</li><li>Full SORP compliance required including use of 'functional headings' on the SOFA.</li></ul>	
> £6.5 million	Accounts must include cashflow statement.	

See the text for explanation of terms used in this table.

* *For accounting years starting on or after 1 April 2011, the £100,000 R&P limit is due to increase to £250,000 and the £2.8 million assets limit is due to increase to £3.26 million – see Appendix for details.*

The requirements in this table apply to all charities registered with OSCR even if based outside Scotland – see UK-wide issues in chapter 1.

Table 2.5 Minimum accounting requirements for charities in Northern Ireland

Income of charity	Minimum requirements regardless of assets*
All charities	• Must apply to CCNI to be registered. • Must keep proper accounting records (retained for six years). • Must produce an annual report and accounts: the accounts can be on a receipts and payments basis (*except for charitable companies* which must use the accruals basis and SORP format whatever the level of income). • Accounts must be independently examined (see chapter 8). • Must submit accounts to CCNI and to members of the public on request.
> £100,000	• Full accruals accounting required. • Presentation of accounts must comply with regulations – with SOFA, balance sheet and notes (SORP format) – but simplified SOFA headings are permitted. • Independent examiner must be professionally qualified.
> £500,000	• Full audit required. • Full SORP compliance required including use of 'functional headings' on the SOFA.
> £6.5 million	Accounts must include cashflow statement.

See the text for explanation of terms used in this table.

* For charities registered in Northern Ireland, the accounting requirements are not affected by the level of the charity's assets.

The requirements in this table are enacted in the Charities Act (Northern Ireland) 2008 but are not expected to be commenced as a legal requirement until late 2011 – see appendix for details. The table assumes that the final regulations will refer to SORP as elsewhere, but this is not yet finally confirmed. It is also possible that the final regulations could amend the £100,000 limit.

This table only applies to charities established in Northern Ireland and registered directly with CCNI. Eventually charities based elsewhere but operating in Northern Ireland will be included on a separate 'section 167' register with CCNI – these will have different accounting requirements: see UK-wide issues in chapter 1.

In the tables, each level shows the *additional* requirements at that income level; the requirements at the lower levels also apply. The thresholds are based on the total income of the charity for the year, considering all funds and projects together (even if some keep their own books). Under the latest changes, it is no longer necessary to consider expenditure thresholds, or figures from prior years. However, some of the details in the tables, particularly the latest changes for charitable companies, only take effect for accounting years which started on or after 1 April 2009 and the

Northern Ireland rules only start from 2011 – if you are dealing with earlier years, see the Appendix for a summary of the differences. Looking further ahead, more threshold changes are possible.

Note that these are *minimum* requirements at each level. A charity is free to do more if it wishes. For example, a charity with income around £90,000 that is bidding for a grant which would take it over £250,000 may find that producing full SORP-compliant accounts even at the current income level helps to demonstrate that it has the professionalism to expand.

The main difference for charitable companies is that there is no provision for receipts and payments accounts; accruals accounts (see below) must be produced no matter how small the income. However, annual reports and accounts for companies must also comply with company law, which in some cases includes additional requirements beyond the SORP (SORP 2005 includes a section on this issue).

Note that, in Scotland and Northern Ireland, some of the thresholds are lower – in particular even the smallest charities, with income under £25,000, must have their accounts independently examined and must submit them to OSCR or CCNI as appropriate.

Accruals or receipts and payments?

In terms of producing the accounts, the biggest difference is whether to prepare them on a receipts and payments basis or on an accruals basis. For charities that are not companies (including CIOs), the receipts and payments basis is allowed in England up to £250,000 income; above this, or for charitable companies, accruals accounts are compulsory.

It is vital to note that whether you use receipts and payments or accruals, the law has requirements about the presentation of the accounts. For example, even if the income of the charity is within the income range where receipts and payments are allowed, you must produce either:

- receipts and payments accounts complying with the Charities Act; or
- accruals accounts complying with the Act, Regulations and SORP.

In either case, there are two main reports, showing what has come into and gone out of the charity over the year (a 'movements' report), and what is in hand at year end (a 'snapshot' report). The basic requirements are described below – see chapter 7 for further details.

Receipts and payments accounting

(a) Receipts and payments account (broken down by funds).

(b) Statement of assets and liabilities (SOAL) (or a statement of balances if following the Scottish rules).

(c) Notes to the accounts are also needed in Scotland (in England and Wales and Northern Ireland, notes are not legally required with receipts and payments although they can be very helpful).

Accruals accounting

(a) Statement of financial activities (SOFA).

(b) Balance sheet.

(c) Notes to the accounts.

The SOFA was invented specifically for charity accounting: it is basically an income and expenditure account divided into columns for the different types of funds. (The funds are explained in chapter 3; an example SOFA is shown on page 100.) Once people get used to the SOFA they usually find it very helpful in getting a picture of a whole charity. The layout of a charity's SOFA, balance sheet and the various information needed in the notes are covered in some detail in the Regulations and SORP.

With receipts and payments accounts, the rules are less detailed: in general, provided that the different funds are clearly separated, the presentation of the year's receipts and payments is quite flexible (although the rules are more specific in Scotland). But although you do not have to do a full balance sheet with receipts and payments accounts, the charity must be able to produce a list of its assets (things the charity has, for example, money in the bank or items of equipment) and liabilities at year end (for example unpaid bills): hence the need for the SOAL.

Accountants often regard receipts and payments accounting and accruals accounting as distinct worlds, but in a charity many normal transactions, such as receiving a donation or paying wages, will be treated the same in either case. The main differences relate to debtors, creditors and fixed assets.

For example, suppose your charity rents out rooms to other organisations, and had raised a substantial bill for room hire that has not been paid by the year end of 31 March 2009 – this would constitute a debtor in the year end accounts. With receipts and payments accounts, you would simply list the debtor on your SOAL in the 2008/09 accounts, but you would not actually record a receipt until the following year (2009/10), when you were paid.

But with accruals accounts, you would say 'this rent was income earned by the charity in the year 2008/09, and it should thus be included as part of the charity's income on the SOFA for that year' (balanced by a debtor on the balance sheet – because at that stage the money is not in the bank). Then in 2009/10, when the room rents are paid, you would just make a transfer from debtors to bank – you would not show any new income, as the income had already been recorded in 2008/09 (or, to use accountants' language, the income was 'recognised' in the earlier year).

If your charity has incurred significant expenses during the year that have not been paid at year end, you would record a year end creditor on the same lines, using the receipts and payments or accruals approach, as relevant.

Tangible fixed assets are items expected to last several years, for example, buildings, computers or vehicles. With receipts and payments accounting, you would record the whole cost of such an item at the time of purchase (and list it on the SOAL for as long as it was kept). But with accruals accounting, you would show the item on the balance sheet and then *depreciate* it over several years. So on each year's SOFA, only that year's depreciation appears as expenditure, and the cost is thus spread over the expected life of the item.

The idea with accruals accounting is that the accounts are more likely to show a 'true and fair view' of the income that has 'accrued' to the charity for the year and of the expenses incurred in running the charity. Occasionally, if there are few debtors, creditors or fixed assets, the figures will be almost the same, whether you use receipts and payments or accruals. But receipts and payments accounts can sometimes show huge fluctuations from year to year: for example if a grant was paid just before year end one year, and just after year end in the following year, or if one year included the purchase of a large fixed asset. Obviously accruals accounting means a little more work, but it allows much more meaningful comparisons to be made from year to year.

If your income is more than £100,000 (£250,000 in England and Wales) or if your charity is a company, you have no choice, and you must use accruals accounts, with the SORP-format for your final accounts (SOFA, etc.).

Below this limit you have a choice between receipts and payments or accruals, but it is best to be consistent for a number of years. Remember the choice affects both:

- how you record certain transactions (where debtors, creditors or fixed assets are involved); and
- the format in which the final accounts are presented.

However, you must use one approach or the other – it is not possible to choose receipts and payments but then, for example, to include some depreciation in the receipts and payments account. Depreciation is a concept which only applies to accruals accounts, so if you want to include depreciation in the figures, the whole accounts must be on an accruals basis and in SORP format.

Issues of accruals accounting are considered further in chapter 10.

3 Charitable funds

If you were keeping the accounts of a business, apart from certain special professions, you would have just one fund: the profit and loss account. All sales income goes into, and all business expenses are charged to, the profit and loss account. Larger businesses may choose to divide the profit and loss into departments, each with their own cost codes, so they can measure the profitability of each area, but this is purely a matter of internal management. At the end of the year, the profits are added together because they all belong to the same owners or shareholders.

In a charity, matters can be very different. Most charities start with one fund, usually called the general fund, which receives donations and from which the expenses of the charity are paid. The report of this fund forms an income and expenditure account (or a receipts and payments account if you are using receipts and payments accounting). At the level of management accounts, the income and expenditure account in a not-for-profit (NFP) organisation is equivalent to the profit and loss account in a business.

But it is likely that, before long, the charity will have a special appeal (say, for building renovations) or will want to launch a new project, and will start to seek funding specifically for that work.

If this is successful, and grants or donations are received specifically for the new project, then of course the relationship of trust (explained in chapter 1) means that the trustees must ensure the money is only spent on the purposes for which it was given. This requires careful bookkeeping, because clearly the new project needs its own income and expenditure account, separate from that of the general fund, otherwise there is no way of tracking whether money received for the new project is really spent on the purposes intended.

The new project thus needs to be treated as a separate fund in the accounts – a *restricted fund* – because there are restrictions on how it can be used. If money given for the new roof appeal were spent on the charity's general running costs, those who had given to the appeal (whether individuals or large grantmakers) would, rightly, be concerned; they could ask for their money back, and the trustees would be guilty of a breach of trust.

Sooner or later, other special projects and appeals will come along, each of which needs its own restricted fund if it is supported by grants or donations given specifically for that purpose. Even very straightforward local organisations will often have two or three funds; large charities can sometimes find themselves managing hundreds of funds.

What is a fund?

A fund is essentially a pot of money or resources held for specific purposes.

As explained, most charities will have a general fund which can be used for any purpose so long as it is within the charity's overall objects – this is known as an *unrestricted fund*, i.e. there are no external restrictions on it (apart from the requirement that all funds of the charity must be used to support the charity's objects).

Restricted funds are pots of money or resources where there is some external condition on how the fund can be used. The condition could arise in one of two ways:

- from the way you asked for the money in the first place (as in 'please give to our new roof appeal'); or
- from a condition imposed by a funder or donor (as in 'this grant must only be used for the salary of the outreach worker').

Many people use some measure of fund accounting for their personal household finances: if you put aside money into different jars (or different bank accounts) labelled 'holiday money' or 'children's clothes', you are in fact doing fund accounting. In this case, the funds would be classed as *designated funds*, because you have decided to designate each jar for a certain purpose; however, you could in principle raid your holiday fund for another purpose if there was something more urgent. Designated funds, like general funds, are part of the general class of unrestricted funds. But, on the other hand, if someone else has made a condition – for example if your aunt gave you a cheque for your birthday and said 'I want you to spend this on some nice new clothes' – then it would be a restricted fund; spending it on something else would be a breach of trust between you and your aunt.

Quite often charities will want to set aside some money from general funds into a designated fund – for example, many charities with buildings to maintain have a 'repairs fund' and every year make a transfer into it from the general fund. Then, when a major repair arises, hopefully there will be enough in the repairs fund to cover the cost, even though it may be more than they could afford in a single year.

The difference between a designated fund and a restricted fund depends on how the fund came to be set up. If it was an internal decision by the charity trustees to set aside the money, it is a designated fund. If necessary, your trustees could decide that the money was more urgently needed for something else. But if the money was externally given on specific conditions, you cannot use it for something else without getting permission from the donor(s) or funder(s) concerned.

This has implications for fundraising – see chapter 12. Obviously people will often give more generously if they know their money will be used for a specific purpose, and some funders, such as the National Lottery distributors, will only support specific projects, so their grants are always restricted (except perhaps with a start-up grant for a new organisation). But if you allow fundraisers to offer a slightly different project to every supporter, it can become almost impossible to track all the separate funds involved.

There is a further type of fund only found in certain charities, known as a *capital fund* or *endowment fund*. This is even more restricted. Capital (or endowment) funds arise when someone gives money to the charity and says 'I want you to invest this, and use the income for certain purposes, but you mustn't spend the capital'. Many grant-making charities derive most of their resources from capital funds set up by someone who wanted to create a long-term resource that could continue making grants long after their death. But sometimes charities will appeal specifically for an endowment fund: for example, charities raising money for specialist medical equipment often have to raise an endowment fund to provide for the running costs of the equipment. (The terms 'capital fund' and 'endowment fund' mean the same thing, but 'endowment' is usually used where long-term investments are involved.)

In such cases, the income of the capital fund – for example interest or share dividends – is posted to another fund (either restricted or unrestricted) so that the income can be spent on the required purpose. But the value of the capital fund itself can go up or down if the assets in the fund (e.g. shares) change in value over the year.

With receipts and payments accounting, the balance of a fund is just the money in the fund. But with accruals accounting, any fund can comprise a mixture of money and/or other assets and liabilities. So, even if you do not have any endowment funds in the investment sense, you may still need to show capital funds in your accounts if, for example, you received a capital grant to purchase a new building: the balance of the fund would be the value of the building.

Figure 3.1 shows the different types of funds in the way that they are classified by the SORP. Strictly speaking, a normal restricted fund where the income can be spent (within the terms of the restriction) should be called a *restricted income fund*.

Figure 3.1   Types of fund

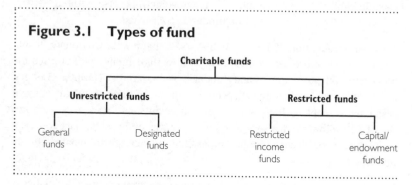

Multi-fund accounting

The need to account for a number of separate funds is probably the biggest issue that distinguishes charity accounting from business accounting.

You may find, for example, that you need many more categories for income and expenditure than you initially thought. It is no good having just one income category for donations: you need to distinguish general (unrestricted) donations, donations for the new roof fund, donations for the outreach fund, and so on. On the expenditure side, if you have staff working on different projects with separate funders, it is no good having one expenditure category for salaries: you need to distinguish general fund salary costs, outreach salary costs, and so on. In practice, every income or expenditure category needs to be clearly labelled with the fund to which it relates.

Provided that your books are structured in this way, it is not too difficult to draw out the relevant figures and produce a separate income and expenditure account for each fund, showing what has come in and what has gone out purely on that fund. You may need this for reporting to funders, but it is also vital so that your trustees can monitor each fund separately. Sometimes a charity will find itself relatively well off in cash terms, but if nearly all the money relates to restricted funds, the position in the general fund may be very tight.

Some charities try to avoid proper fund accounting during the year and leave it to an accountant to sort out at year end. But this can be disastrous: you can easily find you have been spending money that a fund does not have. At the end of the day, if money given for restricted funds has been spent on other purposes, your trustees will have committed a breach of trust.

However, one crucial issue for fund accounting is that a restricted fund will generally continue for more than one accounting year: money given for the new roof or the new outreach worker may not be spent until the next year or later. In that case, in your books you need to be able to work out at year end the balance on the restricted fund (i.e. the income for that fund, less the expenses already incurred) and carry it forward as a restricted 'pot' of resources into next year's accounts. This is clearly very different from the situation described at the start of this chapter, for departments of a business, where all the profits would come together at year end.

Most conventional training for bookkeepers assumes that there will be a single brought forward figure for 'reserves' at the start of an accounting year, but clearly in a charity with more than one fund, you need a *separate figure for each fund* for the balance brought forward at the start of the year. (We will look at the implications of this in chapter 5.) When producing an income and expenditure account for a fund, it needs to show not just the income and expenditure for the year, but also the balance brought into the fund at the start of the year (unless it is a new fund). Similarly, if the project has to continue the following year, you may need the fund to show a substantial balance carried forward at year end, and this needs to be considered when budgeting.

Do we need separate bank accounts?

Many people think fund accounting is easily solved by having a separate bank account for each fund. Sometimes funders seem to imply this, by saying they want their grant held in a separate account, but they usually just mean a separate fund.

However, as you will have seen from the explanation above, provided that your books are properly labelled to show the income and expenditure for each fund, and provided you have a separate 'balance forward' for each fund at year end, you do not need separate bank accounts to keep track of different funds. This is the same whether the accounts are on a receipts and payments or an accruals basis.

In some cases a very small organisation with limited bookkeeping skills may find separate bank accounts helpful. But once you have more than a couple of funds it can become totally unmanageable. If you have reasonable sums in hand at any one time you will probably want a deposit account as well as a current account – this means two bank accounts for each fund. Then, if you need petty cash, you will have to apply the same principle and have a separate petty cash tin for each fund.

It can soon get to the point that a charity with just eight funds will have money held in 24 places. Ensuring that cheques are written on the right account becomes a nightmare. If a bill arrives that needs to be split between more than one fund, you will have to write multiple cheques. Once a cheque is inadvertently written from the wrong account, getting everything sorted out is much worse than managing with one bank account in the first place.

Also, you will normally find you can get much more bank interest if you have one high interest deposit account and just keep enough money in a current account for the short-term requirements of the charity as a whole. (See chapters 4 and 12 for more on managing investments and investment income.)

Similarly, where you need petty cash, one cash tin is fine, so long as all petty cash expenses are clearly marked to show the fund to which they relate (and from a security point of view this is much more manageable).

Transfers between funds

Fund accounting sometimes requires a special transaction in the books – an 'inter-fund transfer'. Clearly this is unique to charity accounting, so you will not find it in normal bookkeeping textbooks.

An inter-fund transfer arises when money or resources need to be transferred from one fund to another. You might feel that this goes against the principles of fund accounting, and certainly such transfers cannot be made on a whim, but there are several situations where such transfers are needed.

We have already considered the case of transferring money from a general fund to a designated fund (for example a fund for long-term repairs); this is a simple example of an inter-fund transfer. However, sometimes trustees will want to transfer funds from the general fund to a restricted fund where a new project is being partly funded by an external grant, but where the charity has agreed to support it partly from general funds.

Trustees cannot, however, restrict money artificially. It is fine to make a funds transfer from unrestricted funds into a restricted fund if it is essential to prevent the restricted fund going into deficit. But if trustees simply wish to put funds aside for a specific purpose the transfer will be made to a designated fund, *not* to a restricted fund.

However, transfers can sometimes be made from a restricted fund to a general fund, if the funder has agreed. For example, the costs of a new project may include a 'management fee' to cover the general overheads of the charity in running the project (for more details see *Managing core costs: full cost recovery*, page 48). If it was clearly agreed with the funder that part of the grant would be spent on these management costs, a transfer of the management fee can be made from the restricted fund to the general fund. (An alternative is to split all costs between funds in the first place, but where funding for a project includes a provision for general overheads, a funds transfer is usually clearer.)

If the different funds are held in the same bank account, a funds transfer is just a 'paper' entry. However it is, of course, a very important entry, and should only be made if specifically agreed by the trustees. In the books, a funds transfer is, in effect, expenditure from one fund which becomes income to another fund – but of course there is no income or expenditure by the charity as a whole.

The importance of this is shown in the year end accounts, where transfers between funds must appear as a separate line on the SOFA (if you are doing accruals accounting), so they are not confused with external income or expenditure (see figure 7.4, on page 100).

4 Financial management and sources of income

In a charity, managing the money is much more than just a matter of good bookkeeping: it is central to the charity's work. In fact, unless you are clear about the sources of your income and how decisions are made about its use, the day to day bookkeeping can be quite meaningless. In a charity, the role of financial management has many features specific to the sector.

Financial responsibility

In a charity, the overall financial responsibility rests with the trustees as a whole. However, in practice, one of the hardest skills for a charity treasurer or finance worker is to enable the trustees to exercise this responsibility effectively so that they take all major financial decisions on an informed basis.

As noted in chapter 2, the trustees have a legal duty to ensure that proper accounting records are kept, but clearly it is impracticable for all trustees to be involved in all the day to day financial transactions of recording receipts, paying bills and salaries, and so on. This must be delegated in some manner.

There are several ways of doing this. It is usual for one of the trustees to be designated as the 'treasurer' of the organisation; within the trustees as a whole he or she will then take particular responsibility for financial issues. Sometimes the term 'honorary treasurer' is used to make it clear that it is a voluntary role. This role can operate in three ways.

- In many small local charities, the treasurer does all the bookkeeping, payment of salaries, liaison with the bank and similar tasks. He or she is personally responsible for producing the year end accounts (or for arranging for this to be done by the auditor or independent examiner) and often handles much correspondence on financial issues, for example arranging insurance.
- In slightly larger charities, a member of staff may be employed (often part-time) to act as bookkeeper, or there is an administrator whose duties include bookkeeping. The usual arrangement is that the treasurer determines the broad financial procedures and the

categories used in the books (see chapter 5), while the bookkeeper handles the detailed work.

In this case the day to day financial procedures are shared between the treasurer and bookkeeper; for example, the treasurer might indicate the type of management report required for the trustees' meeting, but the bookkeeper might produce it.

• In medium-sized and larger charities, it is impossible for a voluntary treasurer to have any more than a broad overview of the financial arrangements. In such cases the paid managers of the organisation are expected to manage the financial affairs, and simply consult the trustees on major financial decisions. There will usually be a senior member of staff with a job title of finance officer or manager or, in organisations operating on a national scale, finance director.

In organisations working on this model, the treasurer's role is less formal, as the finance officer will usually attend trustee meetings and present reports directly. The treasurer will meet with the finance officer from time to time to discuss financial policy, propose formal resolutions of a financial nature at trustees' meetings, and liaise with the auditors on issues at trustee level. But usually such treasurers have limited day to day involvement.

The first model has the advantage of simplicity, but as an organisation grows it can become dragged down by too much dependence on a voluntary treasurer. For example, the key member of staff – the manager – may have no financial information if all books are kept at the treasurer's home, and there may be considerable delays in raising cheques.

However, once a paid bookkeeper is appointed, the relationship between the treasurer and bookkeeper is crucial: the bookkeeper needs the direction of the treasurer on financial procedures; equally, the treasurer needs information from the bookkeeper in order to report to the trustees. This all has to be handled with sensitivity, and if there is a paid manager, the treasurer needs to take care not to treat the bookkeeper as one of his or her own staff.

In the third model the relationship of knowledge may be the other way round. Even a treasurer who is a professional in the accounting or banking world is unlikely to have as much knowledge and experience of charity finance as a full-time charity finance director. The latter may be attending conferences on charity finance and meeting with others in organisations such as the Charity Finance Directors Group. Certainly the treasurer will not have the detailed financial knowledge of the organisation concerned. In such cases, the accountant or finance director may have to take on a gentle educational role, appraising the treasurer of major financial issues affecting the charity.

When it works well, this can be a fruitful relationship, especially if the treasurer takes the lead on difficult issues that would otherwise make the finance officer unpopular. The treasurer of a charity must normally also take the lead on the issue of proposing the remuneration of senior staff.

However, whatever the size of the charity, it is vital that the treasurer and finance staff accept that they are ultimately the servants of the trustees as a whole. Far too many small charities end up with the treasurer alone deciding what can or cannot be afforded. Finance officers can sometimes make the same mistake. It is the responsibility of treasurers or finance officers to advise the trustees, and to give them sufficient information on which to make an informed decision. But financial decisions, like all decisions, must ultimately be made by the trustees as a whole.

Managing the income and expenditure

Most financial management comes down to decisions about income or expenditure, though, as we saw in the last chapter, where a charity has several funds, you need to look at each fund individually.

In general, you might think the key task would be to maximise the income and minimise the expenditure. But in an organisation where you are not seeking to make a profit the task is more complex. Of course you want to avoid wasted expenditure – especially as the charity will usually be spending other people's money – but you are not seeking to get the expenditure as low as possible in order to maximise a profit. Most charities have to spend money in order to advance their charitable objects, so cutting down on worthwhile expenditure actually reduces the charity's effectiveness.

However, it is vital to consider both sides of the income and expenditure account. Where a charity is struggling to make ends meet, there are always two choices – to cut the expenses or increase the income – but often people only consider one or the other. Often the best course is to do some of each.

On the other hand, if the charity (or a certain fund) is doing well and achieving higher income or lower expenses than expected, financial management involves being creative in identifying new areas of expenditure, so that the objects can be further advanced. If you cannot do this, your reserves will just grow (see *Cashflow and reserves*, page 49), perhaps to levels that will bring the charity into criticism. In extreme cases, where income is increasing and there are few ways to spend it, the trustees may need to get the charity's objects changed (in England and Wales this may require applying to the Charity Commission to make a 'scheme', allowing a charity's funds to be applied to new purposes).

However, on a day to day basis, managing expenditure in a charity is not particularly different to any other organisation – setting sensible budgets and monitoring expenses against them is usually the best approach (see chapter 9 for more on management accounts). But the management of income in a charity can involve several issues unique to this sector.

Fundraising

What a charity is able to do to advance its objects is usually constrained by the income that it can generate. It follows that attracting sufficient income is a key role of all charity trustees – this is what is meant by charity fundraising. Curiously, many charities use the term 'fundraising' only to refer to certain types of income generation and some, especially religious charities, object to the word completely. But the term simply means the process of raising or securing sufficient funds to support the work of the charity. So whether you are asking for committed gifts, applying for grants, selling goods or services or maximising investment income, fundraising is all about raising the resources to support the charity's aims.

Some charities will have another trustee who coordinates the fundraising, quite separate from the treasurer, and where staff are employed there may be a paid fundraiser separate from the finance officer. But treasurers and finance officers need to understand the financial implications of different sources of income. (The links between accounting and fundraising are considered further in chapter 12.)

Sources of income

Fundamentally, there are three main ways in which a charity can get income:

- donations
- trading
- investment.

Donated income

Any money given to a charity counts as donated income. As explained in earlier chapters, this ability to attract gifts – often for nothing in return – is at the heart of what it means to be a charity.

Donated income includes any of the following:

- coins or notes placed in a collecting tin or collecting plate;
- a gift from an individual by cheque or standing order or direct debit or by credit card;
- a gift from an individual deducted through their payroll;
- a grant or donation from a charitable trust;
- a grant or donation from a company (provided that it is not seeking anything in return);
- a grant from a local authority or public sector funder (provided that it is genuinely a grant – see below);
- a legacy to the charity in someone's will.

In the case of individual donations to charity, there are very attractive tax rules for direct gifts, payroll gifts and legacies, and with proper understanding of these, a charity can often increase the value of donations considerably (see chapter 12). Some charities make extensive use of gift aid (see chapter 12), for example, but many others are missing out.

Some grants and donations will be for unrestricted funds; others will be tied to specific projects or activities, and thus need to be allocated to restricted funds (or occasionally to a capital fund if it was a capital appeal) (see chapter 3 for an explanation of these terms).

When money is *given* to a charity, the relationship is one of trust. If the money is misused, the trustees could be guilty of a breach of trust and might have to reimburse the funder. Normally there is no contractual relationship. Even if you have a public sector funder that makes a grant with 10 pages of conditions on how it is to be used, it is still a grant to a (very) restricted fund. The funder is not purchasing anything from the charity (if it wants that, it will need a contract – see below).

Some funders like to describe their funding agreements as *service level agreements* (SLAs). You sometimes need to read the small print to work out whether an SLA is actually a grant or a contract, but most are in fact grants (restricted not just in terms of purpose, but restricted also to a certain service level that must be achieved). The Statement of Recommended Practice (SORP) describes grants linked to SLAs as 'performance-related grants'.

Trading income

The second main source of income is trading income – charging for goods or services. When charities get income in this way they are working more like ordinary businesses, but there are still many differences.

Many people think there is some rule preventing charities from trading, but although there are certain limits and tax implications (see chapter 11) trading income is a normal source of income in many charities.

Trading income can include any of the following:

* an educational charity charging fees for places on courses;
* a housing charity charging rents to tenants;
* a charity selling books or publications (where the content is related to the charity's objects);
* a religious charity charging fees for weddings or funerals;
* a counselling charity charging fees for counselling sessions (where a definite charge is made, rather than just asking for a donation);
* a membership charity charging membership fees (where the member gets a definite benefit under the charity's objects – if there is no benefit, the member's subscription is just a donation);
* a health or disability charity charging fees under a contract with the public sector for providing services to people with certain medical conditions.

These would all be referred to as *primary purpose trading*, because what the charity is supplying is directly related to its objects.

For some charities, primary purpose trading is the main source of income. If a funder wants your charity to do work under a contract (rather than a grant) this is a contractual relationship, and the income is trading income. The funder has become a customer, purchasing services, and if the charity fails to deliver the services properly it could be liable for breach of contract. So before entering into major contracts, charities should always review the terms carefully and seek legal advice if in doubt. It is especially important that staff should not be allowed to sign major contracts without approval by the trustees, as a contract may impose long-term obligations.

Trading income also includes:

* selling tickets for a fundraising event;
* selling mugs, tee shirts, cards or souvenirs to raise money;
* selling raffle tickets (this is not a pure donation, because the purchaser may win a prize);

- providing advertising or sponsorship opportunities to companies (where they gain substantial publicity);
- selling second-hand goods in a charity shop or jumble sale;
- selling the charity's services in a way that is outside its objects: for example providing places on courses to people who are outside the charity's beneficiaries, or renting out rooms to commercial organisations.

These are classed as *trading for fundraising purposes* – because what you are supplying is not part of the charity's objects; the reason for the activity is simply to raise funds.

In deciding whether an activity is primary purpose trading or trading for fundraising purposes, the key question to ask is: 'Is the purchaser buying a benefit which is part of the charity's objects to provide?' (e.g. an educational charity selling training) or 'Is the purchaser buying something unrelated to the charity's objects?' (e.g. a souvenir mug or tee shirt). But whenever you are making a charge for something, remember that you are *trading* – you can only treat income as donation if the donor gets nothing significant in return (in the case of gift aid donations there are specific rules on maximum levels of benefit to donors – see chapter 12).

There are few restrictions on primary purpose trading by charities, although VAT sometimes has to be considered. But there are strict limits on trading for fundraising purposes, and above this the charity could be liable to tax (see chapter 11). Activities such as selling raffle (lottery) tickets or selling alcohol also have other legal controls.

In terms of the accounts, primary purpose trading income will normally be posted to unrestricted funds. This can sometimes make a contract more attractive than a grant. You may wish to use a designated fund to keep track of a certain contract funded project, but the charity's obligation is simply to supply the goods or services contracted. If you are able to do this at less than the price agreed, any profit or surplus can be retained by the charity to support the development of services. This is quite different from the trust relationship that applies with grants, where unspent funds may have to be returned. (If you have funders that object to this, and want you to treat their contract as a restricted fund with any surplus being returned to them, ask whether they expect that arrangement with other purchases – for example their stationery suppliers.)

Whilst a surplus on trading income may be attractive, remember that if you have under-costed the work and cannot negotiate an increase in the fee, the charity may still be legally obliged to carry out the work, and you may end up subsidising it from other unrestricted income.

Trading income for fundraising purposes will also usually go to unrestricted funds, unless you specifically asked people to buy tickets or support an event on the basis that the proceeds would be used to support a certain project.

Investment income

Investment income includes any of the following:

- bank interest
- dividends on shares
- rents on investment properties (where a charity holds property specifically for investment purposes – very rare in small charities).

For many local charities the only investment income will be small amounts of bank interest. But for some charities, where there are substantial endowments, investments may be the main source of income; this is the case for many grant-making trusts.

Charities are entitled to a number of tax concessions on investment income: for example interest can be paid gross (you simply need to provide evidence to your bank that the organisation is a charity), and there is no capital gains tax to pay when investments increase in value.

Investment income should normally be allocated to the fund to which the investments belong. In theory, this means that where several funds are held in the same bank account, the bank interest should be split between the different funds on a reasonable basis. However, with normal restricted projects, where the funder expects that the money will be spent fairly soon after receipt, few funders will be that prescriptive, and many charities are thus able to allocate all bank interest to the general fund. Nevertheless, some funders may insist that you seek their permission to take this approach – read the small print of grant agreements. But if you have a long-term appeal such as a building fund, where substantial amounts are raised perhaps a year or more before they can be spent, donors have a right to expect that interest on their donations will be added to the fund concerned.

However, with a capital (endowment) fund, the terms of the endowment will normally require that income is allocated to some other fund. (If the income went back into the endowment fund, the fund would just keep growing and would never be spent on the charity's objects – accounting in this way has prompted Charity Commission investigations.) But with shares and similar investments, take care to distinguish investment income (such as dividends) from capital growth – the latter will remain in the capital fund unless the charity has formal approval for other approaches.

Managing different forms of income

As explained, the trustees have a duty to maximise the income of the charity in order to further its objects and the treasurer or finance officer will usually play a part in implementing this.

With *donated income* the key issue is an effective fundraising strategy. Some charities accept donations passively, but if the work of your charity is worthwhile, you have an obligation to ask people to support it. With grant income, the charity usually needs to be proactive in applying for grants, and plan well ahead where grant income has a finite life.

With *primary purpose trading* the key issue is usually how to price the goods or services you are supplying, and then how to market the service. Since the trade is seeking to advance the charity's objects, you will usually be aiming to break even rather than to make a profit on the activity: generally, keeping the price down will enable you to reach more people. But remember that, unlike business trading, with a charity the customer (the funder) is often quite different from the client or beneficiary who will be using your service. However, if you are offering something that will be paid for directly by your beneficiaries, you may deliberately want to price the service below the cost price, and subsidise it using other income.

With *trading for fundraising purposes*, again pricing and marketing are key issues, but this time the aim is usually to set the price as high as possible (but without putting people off). There is no point in running a fundraising activity that simply breaks even! If people are giving voluntary time to help run an event, the charity needs to make a substantial return to justify their time and effort.

Management of *investment income* is sometimes simply a case of choosing the best deposit account, but for charities with large funds to manage, the management of investments may take up a good part of the time at trustees' meetings. Since the Trustee Act 2000, trustees have much more flexibility in managing investments, but where significant sums are involved they have an obligation to seek professional advice (see chapter 12 for more in this). In such cases, you need to determine an investment policy, which must be stated in the charity's annual report (see chapter 7).

Managing core costs: full cost recovery

Much of the financial management will deal with each fund individually; as explained, you cannot use income to a restricted fund to subsidise deficits elsewhere.

But the relative outcome of each fund is often determined by how overheads (such as the running costs of the charity's premises) are apportioned between funds, or how much you can negotiate in management fees or other contributions to overheads in order to permit transfers from restricted to unrestricted funds.

It is vital to appreciate that, when taking on a new project (for example, involving a new worker), the costs are much more than that person's salary costs and direct project expenses. For example:

- the new person will take up some of the manager's time in supervision;
- he or she will occupy part of your premises (even if the premises are already there, the running costs will usually increase);
- the new worker may need to use the charity's existing equipment (computers, photocopier, possibly vehicles), giving higher maintenance costs;
- the new project will generate additional transactions in your accounts, which may require extra hours for your bookkeeper;
- the extra complexity of the charity's affairs may require additional trustees' meetings;
- the extra income may take the charity over a threshold for its final accounts and thus require extra accountancy fees at year end (see chapter 2);
- if the project finishes and you cannot offer the person other work, you may have to meet redundancy costs;
- the process of bidding for the funds in the first place may have taken up the time of a coordinator or fundraiser.

Different funders have different policies on meeting such costs, and as treasurer or finance officer you need to be aware of these. Some charities find that they can only secure project funding, and unless you can agree a reasonable contribution to overheads from your funders, you may find that you have no unrestricted funds at all. Some funders dislike the term 'management fee' or 'overheads' but are nevertheless willing to pay for a proportion of a manager's time or premises costs as an expense of a project. But obviously your overheads must be reasonable – public sector funders have to consider 'value for money' and a charity seeking to recover the full costs for a well-paid senior manager purely from the overheads of a couple of small projects may find that funders are unsympathetic.

Managing such issues is normally described as 'full cost recovery'. The government has indicated that when public sector bodies purchase services from a charity, they should generally be prepared to pay the *full costs* of the activity, including an appropriate share of overheads. This is also a principle of 'The Compact' (and various local compacts) between the public sector and the voluntary sector.

However, full cost recovery can sometimes be hard to achieve in practice, as public sector funders are often short of resources, and charities are sometimes presented with the stark choice of doing work at less than full cost, or not doing it at all. But a charity should never do work at less than full cost unless this has been explicitly agreed by the trustees. Charity treasurers and finance officers need to be in the lead to ensure that any funding bids are only made on a full cost basis, unless the trustees have clearly agreed to subsidise a project from other income. Sometimes a key task of the treasurer is to support the charity in saying 'no' to a project when funding is insufficient, even if it seems attractive in other ways, if the core costs will not be sufficiently covered.

Cashflow and reserves

In any organisation, it is not enough just to balance income and expenditure, it is also necessary to ensure that there is sufficient money in hand at any one time to meet immediate expenses. Otherwise a charity, like any other organisation, can become insolvent.

Given the uncertainty of much charity income, this management of cashflow often requires more care than in other organisations.

In practice, the difficulties are usually greatest with trading income and with charities whose donated income is subject to major seasonal fluctuations (for example Christmas appeals). In most cases, donated income can be received before the money has to be spent and grants are often paid quarterly or half-yearly in advance. However, some grant programmes are only paid in arrears, i.e. the charity has to incur the expenditure and then claim reimbursement (this is particularly the case with certain forms of European funding). There can also be acute problems if a grant is paid late – some public sector funders are well-known for this.

Projects funded by trading income (or grant income paid in arrears) often require expenditure on salaries or materials before the work can be invoiced, and there may also be a delay of a month or more awaiting payment of the charity's invoice. It is vital to plan for this (see chapter 9 on preparing a cashflow forecast).

Issues of cashflow lead naturally to considering the appropriate level of reserves for a charity – the amount available in general unrestricted funds. (If you are doing accruals accounting, and if the balance of your general fund includes fixed assets, you need to deduct these from the fund balance to get the reserves figure.)

The Charity Commission has had to remind charities from time to time that accumulating money is not itself a charitable purpose. Generally, a charity is expected to spend its income on advancing its objects, unless there is a specific reason for keeping it. There is no problem in retaining money if there is a clear development plan, for example to acquire a new building in a few years' time. But retaining large amounts towards general running costs is not acceptable, this is seen as putting the needs of future (unknown) beneficiaries ahead of current (known) beneficiaries.

There is also a problem that some grantmakers will refuse to help charities with significant reserves; this can encourage inappropriate expenditure prior to year end, just to bring the reserves down to a more acceptable level.

Different charities will need different levels of reserves: a small grant-making charity that only makes one-off grants (i.e. no long-term obligations) may be able to manage with almost no reserves. On the other hand, a service-providing charity running a number of complex projects with uncertain income streams will usually need running costs amounting to at least three months' average expenditure. Where the income is seasonal, or where long-term commitments are made (for example in a charity funding medical research) much higher reserves may be needed.

It is now a requirement of the charity accounting regulations that charity trustees must state their reserves policy in their annual report. This should cover what the trustees feel is a reasonable level of reserves for the charity, how the actual reserves compare with this, and what steps the trustees will be taking to get reserves to a sensible level. This applies even to smaller charities where the year end accounts are on a receipts and payments basis. Usually the policy is expressed in terms of months of expenditure, for example:

The trustees have set a policy of maintaining unrestricted reserves equivalent to six months' expenditure. At present, the reserves amount to just under four months' expenditure, and the trustees will therefore be seeking to increase this in the coming year.

Where the reserves are unacceptably low, it may be necessary for a few years to budget for general fund income to be more than expenditure, until reserves have reached a sensible level, but you need to get supporters to understand the need for this. Conversely, some charities have realised over the years that their reserves have become unnecessarily high, and are now spending them by increasing their activities, so that for a few years their expenditure will be more than their income.

5 Bookkeeping principles

Some people think that bookkeeping is the heart of a treasurer's work and might be surprised to see just one chapter devoted to this. But bookkeeping cannot be done in isolation; you need an appreciation of the issues discussed in the earlier chapters in order to decide where in the books to allocate particular transactions. You also need to consider what will be needed for management accounts (see chapter 9) and final accounts (chapter 7) in order to decide what categories to use in your books.

Who does what?

Effective bookkeeping depends just as much on the human interactions in the process as on the books themselves. Once the charity reaches the size where day to day bookkeeping is done by a member of staff rather than the treasurer, communication between the treasurer, bookkeeper and manager is vital to the task.

Bookkeeping is not just a mechanical exercise: decisions have to be made about what to post where; sometimes a cost has to be apportioned between more than one fund; you need to know if some incoming money is actually a debtor from last year, and so on. Also, new categories and even new funds will need to be added to the books from time to time, such as when the charity receives a grant or donation for a new purpose.

So employing a bookkeeper for just half a day a week, for example, is often not very successful. Such bookkeepers may never really gain sufficient knowledge of the charity to make informed decisions, so they either make assumptions (which often have to be corrected at year end, involving a lot of extra time and cost) or, to do the job properly, they have to ask so many questions that you feel it would be quicker to keep the books yourself. The same problem arises with treasurers who are frequently absent from trustees' meetings.

Also, bear in mind that much of the time of treasurers and bookkeepers is taken up with paying bills, banking receipts, chasing outstanding payments and a whole host of related issues. Actually 'posting transactions' (putting entries in the books) rarely accounts for more than perhaps a quarter of the total time.

In practice, operating any bookkeeping system, whether manual or computerised, can be split into three levels:

1 devising the basic structure of the accounts – drawing up the layout and allocating columns with manual books, or defining a chart of accounts (the list of account headings) in a computer system;

2 posting entries in the books on a day to day basis (together with day to day checks such as bank reconciliation – see chapter 6);

3 closing off the books at the end of an accounting period, working out total figures for each category, and transferring these into appropriate reports for use by others. A very small charity can do this just once a year, but larger charities will usually want monthly or quarterly accounting periods.

Where roles are separated between a treasurer and bookkeeper, the treasurer needs to be involved in levels 1 and 3, but level 2 is usually handled by the bookkeeper alone, except where problems and queries arise. However, an experienced finance officer may handle all three levels, only consulting the treasurer where policy decisions are required.

Format of the books

Clearly, any bookkeeping system must keep a record of all financial transactions affecting the charity. Without a list of individual receipts and payments it is impossible to establish monthly or yearly figures with any certainty.

The simple cashbook

The simplest form of books is just a list of transactions, usually split into columns for receipts and payments.

Date	Cheque no	Details	Receipts	Payments
3 Jan	000271	Rent		250.00
21 Feb	000272	Wages to administrator		83.33
27 Feb	Paid in	Grant from council	2000.00	
12 Mar	000273	Singh & Co – printing		678.00
19 Mar	Paid in	Cash – proceeds of concert	43.90	
21 Mar	000274	Wages to administrator		83.33

Certainly this format keeps a record of transactions. However, it is worth noting that, with systems of this kind, what you write in the 'details' or 'comment' column is vital in order to know at a later date what the transaction was about. A slight improvement, to ensure that you know why each transaction was entered, is to have two narrative columns – one for the name of the payee or funder and one explaining the purpose or reason for the receipt or payment.

Date	Cheque no	Payee/donor	Purpose	Receipts	Payments
3 Jan	000271	ABC Properties	Rent		250.00
21 Feb	000272	R Jones	Admin wages		83.33
27 Feb	Paid in	Midsham Council	Annual grant	2000.00	
12 Mar	000273	Singh & Co	Printing		678.00
19 Mar	Paid in	Cash	Concert proceeds	43.90	
21 Mar	000274	R Jones	Admin wages		83.33

You can draw up this type of layout in any kind of book or on plain paper, although you will find that stationery shops sell a wide range of books already set out in suitable columns. A book has the advantage over separate sheets in that pages are unlikely to get lost, and there is less risk of fraud from someone taking out pages and changing them.

But although this provides a record of transactions, it cannot be said to be a full bookkeeping system, until we look at the issue of 'closing off' the books and adding in whatever funds were in hand at the start of the accounting period.

There are various ways of closing off or 'balancing off' the books at the end of a period. In general, you will want to total the payments and receipts and subtract the payments from the receipts to determine the surplus for the period. You then need to add on the funds in hand at the start of the period, in order to know the balance in hand to carry forward to the next period.

Date	Cheque no	Payee/donor	Purpose	Receipts	Payments
31 Dec	Balance carried forward			373.45	
3 Jan	000271	ABC Properties	Rent		250.00
21 Feb	000272	R Jones	Admin wages		83.33
27 Feb	Paid in	Midsham Council	Annual grant	2000.00	
12 Mar	000273	Singh & Co	Printing		678.00
19 Mar	Paid in	Cash	Concert proceeds	43.90	
21 Mar	000274	R Jones	Admin wages		83.33
31 Mar	Totals for quarter			2043.90	1094.66
	Subtract payments			-1094.66	
	Net surplus for quarter (receipts less payments)			949.24	
	Add on balance brought forward at 31 Dec			373.45	
31 Mar	Balance carried forward			1322.69	

Now that the books have been totalled and closed off, from this simple cashbook you have the figures to produce some helpful management accounts for the quarter for the trustees.

Books like this are quite adequate for a very small charity where everything is done through one bank account and where there are no more than perhaps 30 or so transactions per year. But if you had several hundred transactions, this format would be quite limiting because it does not show in any overall manner from where the income and expenditure has come. Going through a list of more than 100 entries, looking at the purpose of each in order to produce sensible year end accounts, would be a great deal of work.

Analysed cashbook (single fund)

An easy but very useful improvement on the simple cashbook is an analysed cashbook as shown on page 57. Rather than just having single columns for 'receipts' and 'payments' you have a number of columns into which the receipts and payments are analysed. Whenever you post an entry, you take care to write it in the correct column. Most manual bookkeeping systems are based on the use of one or more analysed cashbooks.

Date	Cheque no	Payee/donor	Purpose	Balance forward	Receipts		Payments		
					Grants	Fundraising	Premises	Wages	Print/stationery
31 Dec		Balance carried forward		373.45					
3 Jan	000271	ABC Properties	Rent				250.00		
21 Feb	000272	R Jones	Admin wages					83.33	
27 Feb	Paid in	Midsham Council	Annual grant		2000.00				
12 Mar	000273	Singh & Co	Printing						678.00
19 Mar	Paid in	Cash	Concert			43.90			
21 Mar	000274	R Jones	Admin wages					83.33	
31 Mar		Totals for quarter for each category		373.45	2000.00	43.90	250.00	166.66	678.00
		Total receipts and payments				2043.90			1094.66
		Subtract payments from receipts				-1096.66			
		Net surplus for quarter		949.24		949.24			
31 Mar		Balance carried forward		1322.69					

However, even with just two columns of receipts and three columns of payments it can be difficult to show them on a single page, and in reality most charities will need many more categories of income and expenditure. Some people combine the 'Balance forward' column with another column, but it is clearer if you can keep it separate.

The best way of creating more space is to keep two separate cashbooks, one for receipts and one for payments (see pages 59–60). Both the receipts and payments must, of course, be closed off at the same date.

It is possible to buy books with around 16 columns, across a double page spread. Some columns will be used for dates, descriptions and cheque numbers, so it is usually possible to have up to about 12 columns for financial analysis. With separate books for receipts and payments, this will give you around 12 income categories and 12 expenditure categories.

However, one advantage of the simple cashbook and analysed cashbooks above is that it is quite easy, if you wish, to add an extra column for the running bank balance (in the second example, you could use the balance forward column). Once you keep receipts and payments on separate pages, you will find this more difficult. But this is not necessarily a problem if you can keep the bank balance somewhere else, such as a running balance on cheque stubs.

Analysed cashbook (multiple funds)

However, in many charities the bookkeeping must distinguish several funds. This means considerably more columns because, as explained in chapter 3, you must be able to distinguish receipts and payments for each fund. However, if you have no more than two or three funds, and if you do not need too many categories for each, you can still work with two analysed cashbooks – one for receipts and one for payments.

In such cases, remember that you need a separate balance forward for *each* fund – this is usually shown in the receipts book.

RECEIPTS BOOK

Date	Receipt ref	From	Purpose	GENERAL FUND				OUTREACH FUND		
				Balance forward	Grants	Fund-raising	Interest	Balance forward	Grants	Participation fees
31 Dec		Balances carried forward		373.45				0.00		
14 Jan	Deposit	Midsham Trust	Outreach grant						800.00	
27 Feb	DC	Midsham Council	General grant		2000.00					
3 Mar	Deposit	Cash	Concert			43.90				
19 Mar	Deposit	Cash	Outing							24.00
30 Mar	Int	Midwest Bank	Interest Jan–Mar				3.27			
31 Mar		Totals for quarter for each category		373.45	2000.00	43.90	3.27	0.00	800.00	24.00
		Total receipts for each fund					2047.17			824.00
		Subtract payments (from PAYMENTS book)					-1109.66			-591.21
		Net surplus for quarter for each fund		937.51			937.51	232.79		232.79
31 Mar		Balances carried forward		1310.96				232.79		

PAYMENTS BOOK

Date	Cheque No	Payee	Purpose	GENERAL FUND				OUTREACH FUND		
				Premises	Wages	Print/ stationery	Trustees	Wages	Travel	Activities
3 Jan	000271	ABC Properties	Rent	250.00						
21 Feb	000272	R Jones	Admin wages		83.33					
21 Feb	000273	J Smiley	Outreach wages					230.00		
27 Feb	000274	K Patel	Travel expenses				15.00			
3 Mar	000275	K Patel	Outreach travel						49.84	
12 Mar	000276	Singh & Co	Printing x 2			678.00				
17 Mar	DD	ABC Hire	Play equipment hire							52.00
21 Mar	000277	R Jones	Admin wages		83.33					
21 Mar	000278	J Smiley	Outreach wages					230.00		29.37
31 Mar			Totals for quarter for each category	250.00	166.66	678.00	15.00	460.00	49.84	81.37
			Total payments for each fund				1109.66			591.21
1 Apr			*(Start of payments for next quarter)*							

Cashbooks for each fund

If you have more than two or three funds, or if you find you need the whole page width to cover all the categories for just one fund, the only solution is to keep separate books for each fund.

Many charities do this, but great care is needed with a transaction that is split across funds. In the example on page 60 the printers Singh & Co have clearly invoiced two printing jobs together – one relating to the General Fund and the other to Outreach – and a single cheque number 000276 has been written for £730 to cover this. But the cost is split into separate columns: £678 to 'General Fund printing and stationery' and £52 to 'Outreach activities'. On a single page, it is fairly easy to read across the line, but with separate books, extensive cross referencing is needed in such cases.

This shows the limits of single entry bookkeeping, and if you have split transactions arising regularly, double entry bookkeeping (see page 63) is to be recommended.

Multiple bank accounts and petty cash

The examples above assume that all receipts and payments go into a single bank account. This certainly keeps things simple, because your books do not need to show where a receipt is paid into, or on which account a cheque is written. If you can bank all receipts as soon as they arrive and make all payments by cheque or electronic transfer, it is much easier than keeping temporary amounts in petty cash.

Deposit accounts

Many charities will need a deposit account of some kind, but provided that this is only used for transfers to and from the current account, it does not add any great complication. Normal receipts and payments will go via the current account, so the main cashbook is unaffected.

It is helpful to keep a separate note of the running balance of the deposit account, with details of transfers in and out (just as you will, hopefully, keep a running balance for the current account – e.g. in the cheque book). But if you are keeping accounts broken down by fund (as required for charities), rather than broken down by bank account, transfers to or from the deposit account do *not* appear in the payments or receipts. You are simply transferring the assets of the charity from one account to another, but the charity has not actually received any new funds or paid anything out.

When you receive interest on the deposit account, remember that you need to post this in the books as a receipt, and it is easiest if the bank will agree to pay deposit account interest into the current account. If not, remember that deposit account interest needs recording both in the receipts book and in your record of deposit account movements.

Handling multiple cheque accounts and petty cash

If you sometimes pay large cheques directly into the deposit account, or if you have more than one account on which cheques can be written, your books need to be more elaborate. This is also the case if you keep money in, and sometimes make payments directly from, petty cash.

The best way to treat petty cash is just like another bank account. So when you draw money from the bank for petty cash, remember that no money is going out of the charity even though you are writing a cheque: it is just like transferring assets between current and deposit accounts. It is only when you spend petty cash that you have payments to enter in the payments book.

Some people make the mistake of simply adding an extra column to the payments book for 'Petty cash drawn', but of course this does not explain the *purpose* of the expenditure and, in any case, not all the petty cash drawn will necessarily be spent. At year end, if all the petty cash expenses have been lumped into one column, a lot of work is needed to go through petty cash books and break down the expenditure: it is much better to do this during the year as petty cash is spent. Also, with a bank account you can rely on the bank to keep certain records, but with petty cash it is all down to you. So, as well as your normal books, it is vital to have a system of petty cash vouchers or a petty cash book where cash expenses are immediately noted. From time to time (perhaps once a month) you can transfer the total petty cash expenses into the main payments book, split into columns as required.

If you take in cash receipts (for example from collections, events or charity shops) it is usually best to bank the receipts gross, and deal with petty cash expenses separately. If you start reimbursing expenses out of cash received it needs very thorough bookkeeping to keep track of what is happening and to satisfy your auditor or examiner.

Many people think petty cash accounting is simple, but in fact it makes life a lot more complicated. It needs considerably more skills to keep accounts correctly in an organisation where petty cash is widely used. It is much easier if small expenses can be met personally by staff or trustees and then reimbursed promptly by cheque or bank transfer. Provided that you devise a proper expense claim form for such cases, this is much easier to trace.

To handle receipts and payments made directly from petty cash, or where there is more than one bank account, you need an extra column in your payments and receipts books to show which account has been used in each case. But it then becomes much harder to reconcile your receipts and payments to your bank accounts. To be sure your figures are correct, you really need to keep a running balance for *each* bank account and *each* petty cash account (and be sure to check regularly that the figure in your book for the petty cash balance agrees to the physical amount in the box).

Once you do this, you are effectively posting every transaction into two places in your books (or 'ledgers' as they are sometimes called) – to the receipts or payments ledger and to the bank or petty cash ledger (you need a separate bank/petty cash ledger for each bank account and each pot of petty cash). This is called *double entry bookkeeping*.

Double entry bookkeeping

The bookkeeping systems shown in the previous illustrations are all single entry systems, where each amount is written in one place only. But professional bookkeepers will normally use double entry bookkeeping, where everything is written in two places.

Double entry bookkeeping involves more work, but it has the advantage that it can cope even with very complex systems, and its internal checks help to detect errors. Even if you have seven bank accounts, three petty cash accounts, 15 funds with 40 or more income and expenditure categories in each fund, reliable manual books can be kept on a double entry basis.

The concept of double entry bookkeeping relies on having a number of ledgers, each with two columns, called 'debits' and 'credits'. So rather than trying to have vast numbers of columns across the page, you keep each account as a separate ledger. These can be done in a book with two columns per page (plus space for dates and comments) and a separate page for each ledger. (Note that with fund accounting, you cannot have just one ledger for a fund: you need a separate ledger for each income category and each expenditure category of the fund.)

Any transaction always involves at least two postings: a debit to one account and a credit to another account. (In a split case, you could have two or more credits adding up to a single debit or vice versa, but the debits and credits must always balance.)

Here are some simple examples of double entry transactions:

- £2,000 General Fund grant received and paid into bank
  - Debit: Bank £2,000
  - Credit: General Fund grant income £2,000
- £730 Printing bill paid (split between two funds)
  - Credit: Bank £730
  - Debit: General Fund printing/stationery £678
  - Debit: Outreach Fund activities £52
- £150 Petty cash drawn (cheque written for cash)
  - Credit: Bank £150
  - Debit: Petty cash £150

People sometimes query why you debit the bank when receiving money, and credit it when paying out: this is the opposite to what you see on bank statements. But the whole concept of debits and credits relates to the notion of debtors and creditors (see chapter 10), and if two people enter into a transaction, one person's debtor is another person's creditor. Banks generally produce statements in terms of *their* books – not yours!

So if you deposit money at the bank, from the bank's point of view it is not their money – it is money they owe to you – so in their books it is a creditor, and they show the entry as a credit. But in your books, the bank has money which belongs to you – to you the bank is a debtor. In your books, paying money into the bank is increasing the bank's debts to you, so you post it as a debit. (Think about it in a dark room for a few minutes!)

The same applies with normal commercial transactions. If A sells something to B on an invoice (which is not yet paid), the amount due is a debtor in A's books, but in B's books the amount payable is a creditor. (This is taking us into accruals accounting – see chapter 10. But even with receipts and payments accounting, double entry bookkeeping is very useful if you have several funds or several bank accounts.)

Any double entry system allows you to do a very useful check called a *trial balance*. This means adding up the net balance on every ledger (debits less credits or vice versa) and putting them down as a list. Because the debits and credits have to balance for every transaction, it follows that total debits and total credits should be the same across all the accounts. If you find that they are not, you must have misposted a double entry somewhere.

To run a proper double entry system manually, you can in principle post everything directly to the two ledgers concerned. But because of the risk of posting one half of a double entry and then getting distracted before you have done the second half, it is often best to write everything in a simple cashbook first, and then post from there into the ledgers.

In a book of this length there is no space to explain all the details of double entry bookkeeping, but nowadays very few charities (or businesses) do full double entry bookkeeping on a manual basis. Most computer-based accounting systems work internally on a double entry basis (with the guarantee that the debits and credits balance). Also, at year end, your auditor or examiner may ask you to post adjustments in your accounts, which they will usually give to you as a list of debits and credits (special transactions of this kind are often called 'journals'). So, whilst few treasurers and administrators are experts in double entry bookkeeping, it is useful to have a general appreciation of how it works.

Manual books or computers?

Although it is possible to keep even quite complex books on a manual basis, nowadays most charities start to consider computerising their accounts once there are too many categories for an analysed cashbook. Access to computers is rarely a problem today, but just having a PC is not enough; it is important to think about suitable software.

There are three levels of using computers in charity accounting:

- spreadsheets
- general purpose accounting systems
- charity-specific accounting systems.

Spreadsheets

A spreadsheet, such as Microsoft Excel or Corel Quattro Pro, allows you to maintain complex financial data in rows and columns, within 'cells'. It can provide more columns than you can get across the page of a normal cashbook, and can total the columns for you automatically. Many people use spreadsheets for bookkeeping and at first sight – particularly if you already have some experience of using a product such as Excel for other purposes – you might feel that this is the obvious approach.

But spreadsheets have some serious disadvantages if you are trying to set up a complete bookkeeping system. When you open a spreadsheet you have access to all the cells at once, and even in a modest charity with (say) 50 income and expenditure categories (over a number of funds) and 500 transactions per year, your spreadsheet will have 25,000 cells. The size makes it cumbersome and hard to manage, with a great risk of putting entries in the wrong cell. Moreover, unlike manual books – where corrections are easily spotted if you write the books in ink – there is nothing in a spreadsheet to stop someone changing something entered earlier in the year, so it is easy to wipe out earlier entries that have been checked and balanced.

Also, many people who use spreadsheets for bookkeeping are just keeping a single entry analysed cashbook – often there is no corresponding record of running balances on bank accounts, petty cash, etc., so there is often no means of doing bank reconciliation from the spreadsheet figures.

If you are an expert spreadsheet user some of these issues can be overcome, but this may almost mean writing your own accounting system in spreadsheet macros (in fact some accounting systems run essentially as applications within Excel, but this is very different to using a spreadsheet of your own devising). Few charities concerned about financial management therefore rely on spreadsheets as their sole means of bookkeeping, and those that attempt it usually end up keeping extensive manual books as well.

The real value of spreadsheets is not for bookkeeping, but for financial analysis, management accounts, budgeting for new projects and the like. They can also allow you to take figures from your accounts and present them in attractive graphical ways. Many accounting systems allow you to export figures to a spreadsheet for this purpose.

General purpose accounting systems

If you wish to keep reliable books of account, an accounting system is much better than a spreadsheet. Computer-based accounting systems allow you, firstly, to define the individual accounts (or ledgers) into which you want your accounts broken down, and then to post transactions using simple methods of input. Because of this, they can maintain an *audit trail* – a list of transactions and where they were allocated – and most such systems use double entry bookkeeping (although, except for journal transactions, you do not usually have to know about debits and credits).

The audit trail means that it is possible to trace with certainty how the final figures are reached. Moreover, you can be certain when posting an entry that it will only affect the accounts intended. You can usually have as many accounts as you wish (or if there is a limit it is very large) – you are not limited to the columns on a page.

Accounting systems do not necessarily save time in terms of recording transactions in the first place: it takes about as long to enter a transaction in a computer-based accounting system as it does to write it in a book. But the major benefit of computer-based accounting systems is that they will produce a wide range of reports automatically from the transactions entered. You can usually print a profit and loss account or balance sheet within a few seconds, and you can do this at any time; whereas with manual books it is very difficult to produce reports except when the books are periodically balanced off.

Of course, any computer system needs time to learn, and care is needed in setting up a sensible chart of accounts in the first place (you may need training to help with this). There is also the risk that if your computer fails, you could lose the whole year's accounts, so it is vital to take regular backups of the files. But this is, in fact, a great advantage of computer systems; the data can quickly and easily be backed up when needed, and the backups can then be taken off site so you could still recover the data even in the event of a fire or flood. With manual books, to make an off-site backup you would have to photocopy every page.

Compared with manual books, computer-based accounting systems thus offer several advantages:

- much better financial information and reports available at any time;
- ability to handle many more categories than are (easily) possible with manual books;
- a huge time saving at end of quarter and end of year;

- a reliable audit trail (no risk of imbalanced double entries, for example);
- much easier to make security backups.

With larger and more complex general purpose accounting systems, it may be possible to define your own reports to help make them more charity-specific, but this needs a lot of setting up and you will probably need a fairly sophisticated product.

Charity-specific accounting systems

Most smaller general purpose accounting systems are based around the idea of small business accounts (or sometimes domestic household accounts). So although they will keep your transactions and post them to ledgers, it may take a lot of work at year end to get the accounts into the form you need, and you may need help from an accountant. In practice, charities using general purpose accounting systems often rely heavily on downloading information into spreadsheets, and then use some spreadsheet manipulations to get what they need. This requires a lot of skill, both with the accounting system and the spreadsheet.

One of the key issues is usually fund accounting. As explained in chapter 3, this is quite different from departments within a business, because you need a separate balance forward on each fund. It is vital that you can determine the balance of any fund at any time without a lot of work. A number of general purpose accounting systems do have some means of handling fund accounting – they may not use this term but there may be some other facility (e.g. 'classes') which allows you to divide the accounts into funds, rather just a single profit and loss account – but of course you must have a proper understanding of such features before attempting to define your chart of accounts.

Also, some general purpose accounting systems have specific add-on modules for charity accounting: as well as handling fund accounting, this may include facilities such as the ability to produce a statement of financial activities (SOFA – see chapter 7); if the structure of your accounts is directly linked to this, the process is much easier.

However, there are some accounting systems designed specifically for the charity sector (different products being aimed at different sized organisations). At the smaller end, even if your charity only plans to do receipts and payments accounts, a simple accounting system that handles multiple funds using double entry bookkeeping, with the ability to produce a receipts and payments account for each fund, is far better than relying on spreadsheets. But for organisations with more complex needs, charity-specific systems may be available which can handle multiple levels of coding (e.g. by projects, funds and activities) with project reporting across multiple years, and may even offer facilities such as partially-exempt VAT calculations (see chapter 11).

Whether you choose a general purpose or specialist accounting system, you will be making a considerable investment of time in getting a system set up and working. So it is important to consider what support you will get in the event of problems and queries (sometimes this can cost more than the software). Will you be dealing with people who have any charity-specific understanding if, for example, you need guidance on an inter-fund transfer? Also, if the system has documentation written specifically for charities, this can be much easier than trying to set up a system using manuals or help features that assume you are running a business.

Posting interest, direct debits and similar items

Any bookkeeping system, whether manual or computerised, must show *all* financial transactions – including those that happen without your involvement at the time.

You will not necessarily know about every transaction in order to post it immediately when it occurred – for example things such as bank interest, direct debits and bank charges may not be known until you receive a bank statement. This can also apply to income paid directly into your account, for example from funders or regular donors, or gift aid tax refunds from HM Revenue & Customs (HMRC) (see page 162). In such cases, wait until you get the statement and then post these items in the books before closing off the accounts. In fact, it is always a good idea to do bank reconciliation before closing the books, so you can correct any erroneous postings (see page 84 for more on *Bank reconciliation*).

You may need to ask your bank to let you have statements at dates that tie up with your accounting periods when you want to close off your books. (Online banking can ease this problem, but do make sure the security arrangements are adequate – see chapter 6.)

Bank interest is posted in the books as a normal receipt. Direct debits need entering as normal payments (remember that although a direct debit is a debit in the bank's books, with double entry bookkeeping it will be a credit in your books). If you have incoming standing orders – perhaps for regular donations – enter them as receipts, though if you have a separate database for fundraising records it is usually best to enter incoming standing orders first in the fundraising system, and then transfer just a weekly or monthly total into the main accounts (rather than recording everything in two places).

Because you may have to wait for a bank statement to post these items, the entries in your books will not necessarily be in precise date order, but the date in the books should always relate to the original transaction (e.g. the date when the cheque was written, or the date the money came into your account). These entries will not have cheque numbers to show the books, so use codes such as 'DD' (direct debit), 'DC' (direct credit), 'Auto' (automatic payment), 'Int' (interest), 'SO' (standing order) and so on, to make the entry clear.

Posting wages and salaries

For many treasurers, the normal entry of receipts and payments is not too difficult, but wages and salaries can present particular problems because of the rules on tax, national insurance (NI) and other deductions.

Of course, you cannot post salary payments in your accounts until the basic PAYE (Pay As You Earn) calculations have been done. The tasks of a treasurer or finance officer may include operating a PAYE system for the charity. However, PAYE is not particularly charity-specific: apart from the importance of understanding the distinctions between staff and volunteers, PAYE principles are the same for any organisation employing staff. Plenty of guidance is available both from books (see *Further reading*) and from the HMRC website, and many local HMRC offices offer training for businesses (including charities) taking on staff for the first time.

PAYE calculations have to be done each time wages or salaries are paid. They can be done manually (using the forms provided by HMRC), or be computerised (if you have a number of staff) or contracted out. Many local charities use the services of an umbrella body such as a local infrastructure organisation or a diocesan office to do their PAYE calculations.

Once the PAYE calculations are done, there are generally two payments to make – a net payment to the employee and a payment of taxes and NI to HMRC (Collector of Taxes). But the numbers can be quite confusing because there are three separate taxes: the employee's income tax (deducted from his/her salary); the *employee's* NI (also deducted from the salary) and the *employer's* NI, which has to be paid by all employers (including charities) on top of the gross salary due to the employee.

The diagram below shows a possible case (with hypothetical numbers). The employee has earned £1,000 salary this month, from which you must deduct tax (£200 in this case) and employee's NI (£80). So the actual salary cheque – or the amount paid by bank transfer if used – is £720. You must then pay these deductions to the Collector of Taxes (HMRC), together with the £100 of employer's NI on top of the salary. So the total payment to HMRC in this example is £380.

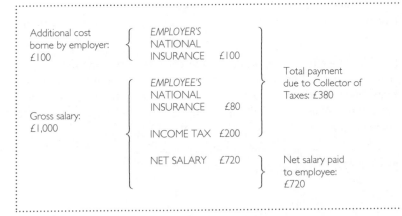

The two payments – £720 to the employee and £380 to HMRC – add up to £1,100, which is the total cost of employing the person that month, and if both are paid immediately you will write two cheques. If you have other deductions such as pension contributions (including stakeholder pensions), or payroll giving (for donations to charity), the same general principles apply, and you may then be making three or four payments in all, for example, to the:

- employee
- HMRC
- pension provider
- payroll-giving agency.

It is generally best to post each payment as a separate entry in the books, although if you understand journals it is possible to post an entire month's payroll as a single journal – but be sure to keep a detailed note of how you arrived at the figures.

Other deductions and adjustments can arise: in particular, student loan repayments (the amounts are deducted from salary and paid through HMRC with the tax and NI) or tax credits (which work like a negative tax so they *increase* a person's pay). If you are employing staff entitled to tax credits and you have little tax and NI to deduct, you may be in the position where HMRC is giving you a net refund in order for you to pay tax credits on top of salaries. Similar issues can arise when employees are entitled to Statutory Sick Pay, Statutory Maternity Pay, Statutory Paternity Pay or Statutory Adoption Pay. Small employers can recover 100% of these costs from HMRC, but for a charity with a large payroll you may only get 90–92% reimbursed (the limits vary from year to year) – so the difference has to be treated as an expense met by the charity. If you have employees affected by any of these issues you will almost certainly want to use payroll software to do the calculations.

Some organisations like to allocate the employer's NI (and any pension contributions paid by the employer) to a different account from the gross salary in order to distinguish 'on costs' from direct salary. In order to get the correct totals, this would need the following postings (expressed in double entry format):

- £720 Net salary cheque
  - – Credit: Bank £720
  - – Debit: Salary expenditure £720
- £380 Collector of Taxes cheque
  - – Credit: Bank £380
  - – Debit: Salary expenditure £280
  -   Debit: Employer's NI expenditure £100

Where salary costs have to be split between two accounts – perhaps because a member of staff is splitting their time between two projects – apportion both the net salary payment and the HMRC payment on the same formula. If you want your books to be linked directly to the format of the SOFA (see chapter 7), you may also need to split salary costs between time spent on direct charitable activities as opposed to time spent on generating funds or on governance work. But if you need to do apportionments like this, try to avoid also splitting out the employer's NI, or the whole process could become unmanageable.

If you have several employees you can make a single payment to HMRC, to cover the tax and NI for all staff. If you do this, take care to allocate the costs for each employee to the correct expenditure accounts.

The payment to HMRC does not have to be made until the 19th of the following month (or 22nd if paid electronically), so at year end this can mean that quite a large creditor is outstanding in your accounts. In fact, small organisations (those whose average monthly tax and NI is less than £1,500) can opt to pay the tax and NI just once a quarter, which means there will nearly always be some tax and NI waiting to be paid.

To show this properly you really need to use accruals accounting (see chapter 10) with the tax amount entered as a creditor. So, in the example above, at the time of doing the payroll you would post:

- £380 HMRC amount due
  - – Credit: Creditor (tax and NI) £380
  - – Debit: Salary expenditure £280
  - – Debit: Employer's NI expenditure £100

and then when the payment is made (possibly in the following year) the entry will be:

- £380 creditor paid by cheque to HMRC
  - – Credit: Bank £380
  - – Debit: Creditor (tax and NI) £380

If you do not want to get into this, the simplest way is to pay all the tax and NI to HMRC before the end of the month; you can then use normal payments – as in the first example, on page 72).

Posting non-bank transactions

The vast majority of transactions in your books will be receipts and payments of some kind, or possibly transfers of money between bank accounts. If you forget to enter any of these you will soon realise when you do a bank reconciliation (see pages 84–85).

But some transactions arise purely from policy decisions, or from knowledge of amounts outstanding, and are thus easily overlooked.

Before you close the books at the end of an accounting period, you need some means of checking with others whether any non-bank entries are needed.

A transfer between funds (see chapter 3) is, in effect, a payment from one fund and a receipt into another fund, but if the funds share the same bank account, no bank entry is involved. Or in double entry terms:

- £500 transfer from General Fund to Outreach Fund
  - Debit: General Fund expenditure 'Transfers *to* other funds' £500
  - Credit: Outreach Fund income 'Transfers *from* other funds' £500

It is best to post fund transfers to columns or accounts separately from other receipts and payments, so that they can be separated as inter-fund transfers on the SOFA, and are not confused with external receipts or payments.

If you are keeping accruals accounts, you will also need a wide range of other non-bank postings, in order to enter debtors, creditors, depreciation and so on (see chapter 10). With receipts and payments accounts, these do not have to be entered in the monetary books, but you still need to have some means of tracking debtors, creditors and fixed assets – a paper list may be sufficient – so you can include them on the statement of assets and liabilities (SOAL – see chapter 7).

Changing the currency of the books

One important issue to bear in mind that may have a major impact on bookkeeping is the possibility that at some stage the UK may join the single European currency (the euro).

At the time of writing this has been ruled out for the next few years, but the official position is still that UK should be ready to join the euro when the conditions are right. Hence, government advice is that any organisation handling money should be able to handle a euro changeover. HM Treasury's Euro Preparations Unit (which has an advisory panel that includes the voluntary sector) publishes a range of guidance. This is based on the 'National Changeover Plan', under which organisations should be ready for full adoption of the euro as the retail currency in the UK within 30 months of a successful referendum.

Whatever your personal views, if this happens, your charity needs to be able to handle the changeover without huge additional costs. The period of 30 months' notice ($2\frac{1}{2}$ years) is well within the life of most computer systems, and so any charity purchasing new accounting software would be well advised to ensure it is euro-ready.

Initially you may find that coping with awkward amounts is the biggest challenge: a regular incoming donation of £20.00 per month might change to something awkward like €28.86 (the actual conversion rate will be fixed, but will involve up to six decimal places, so rounding will be needed).

Local charities will not need multi-currency accounting: you would simply change everything from pounds to euro as from a certain date (use the same date as when your bank account is converted). But bear in mind the changeover may not coincide with your accounting year end (the government proposes that the changeover date for the UK would be 6 April, i.e. the start of the new tax year, in whatever year is chosen). All reports after the changeover will need to be in euros, even though they may partly include periods when you were still working in pounds. Even after the change, you would probably still receive some cash donations in sterling.

Changing from keeping accounts in pounds to euros will obviously have a huge effect on the accounts in any kind of organisation. There will be plenty of guidance, and the experience of voluntary organisations in other countries that have already been through a euro changeover is helpful. But most charities are long-term organisations and it is worth building this into your plans.

6 Checks and controls

Bookkeeping procedures, as discussed in the last chapter, are only useful if people are confident about them. A key question for the trustees of any charity (and for its donors, funders, members and others) is: 'do the books properly record all the income due to the charity and all expenditure as agreed by the trustees?'

To some extent this will be answered at year end by the charity's independent examiner or auditor – see chapter 8. But examiners and auditors rely heavily on the internal controls built into your own systems: if you want your auditors to examine every item of expenditure individually and check whether it has been approved by trustees and posted to the correct fund, you will have to pay an astronomical audit fee. In any case, the trustees have a legal duty to keep proper records, and the examiner or auditor will want assurances from the trustees that they have done so; it is difficult to give such an assurance unless the trustees are confident that proper checks and controls are working.

Moreover, if there are problems in the books, you want to know about them before year end; for example if a fraud was going on but was not uncovered until after year end, a great deal of money could have been lost. At a lesser level, any treasurer or bookkeeper will make occasional mistakes, and the more these can be picked up through simple checks, the better the quality of the financial information obtained from the accounts.

Approval of expenditure

In a tiny charity, every payment might be discussed individually at a trustees' meeting, and the cheques written and signed at the meeting. But most organisations need to delegate decisions for approving day to day expenses and writing cheques.

However, these procedures need to be clear and robust, otherwise there is a serious risk of the charity's funds being spent on non-charitable purposes or on costs that are not intended or agreed. Moreover, with multiple funds (see chapter 3) you need to ensure that expenditure is considered separately in relation to each relevant fund, and then posted to the correct fund in the books.

Controls on signing cheques and other payments

A basic requirement now widely accepted in charitable organisations of all sizes is to ensure that all cheques have to be signed by two people – normally two trustees. The Charity Commission expects charities to have such controls, and many funders impose similar conditions on organisations applying for grants. Other arrangements are generally acceptable for smaller amounts if the bank will accept formal instructions with different levels of signing. For example, a charity with eight staff and £200,000 income might use the following:

- cheques or other one-off payments up to £500 – one signature required, signatory can be a senior member of staff or a trustee;
- cheques or one-off payments £500 to £10,000 – two signatures of which at least one must be a trustee;
- cheques of £10,000 and above or any recurring payments (standing orders/direct debits) – must be signed by two trustees.

The very largest payments should always require two trustees' signatures – and for the controls to work, the bank must be willing to follow these rules for *all* payments going out of the account, not just cheques. But you must ensure such arrangements are permitted by your governing document; if your constitution or trust deed says 'all cheques must be signed by two trustees', you must keep to this.

Some organisations find it difficult to get two signatories that include at least one trustee, and they try to find ways round it. But provided that you have three or four signatories (on an 'any two out of four' basis), you should usually be able to get cheques signed within a few days, even if they have to go by post between signatories.

Many banks now offer online banking systems whereby electronic payments can be approved remotely by signatories over the Internet. For example, a payment can be raised by a finance officer, which generates an email to the signatories, but the payment will not be released until two separate trustees have each clicked on an appropriate weblink to authorise the transaction and entered a personal password. Charities should be very wary of using online or telephone banking without such controls – any system that allows one person to approve payments without an upper limit is not suitable. Also, great care needs to be taken over Internet security and passwords – most people receive numerous bogus 'phishing' emails pretending to be from banks, and an inexperienced staff member or trustee can easily be fooled.

All payments should, of course, be approved by two *independent* signatories. So, for payments such as reimbursing trustees' expenses, the trustee being paid should not be one of the signatories (unless that specific payment has been discussed by the trustees as a whole).

However, where a charity has separate current and deposit accounts, it is often helpful if the treasurer or finance officer can make transfers between accounts held at the same bank without trustees' approval and without anyone else having to sign. No money is going outside the charity in such cases, and this flexibility can allow the charity to get as much interest as possible on any funds not needed immediately.

Where a charity has investments, similar arrangements may be appropriate for small transfers, but the trustees must remain responsible for investment policy, and hence they should not allow major investment decisions to be made by one person.

The role of the second signatory

Having cheques or electronic payments authorised by two people only offers protection if both signatories give careful thought before signing. For one person to pre-sign cheques before they are completed, or even to sign completed cheques without any real thought, offers no protection at all.

Suppose you are the second trustee authorised to sign cheques and the treasurer presents you a cheque or electronic payment for countersignature; it is worth asking these questions before signing.

- Is the payment for a definite bill or invoice? If so, be sure you see the bill and check the amount and the payee before signing.
- Does the bill relate to expenditure of a kind that the trustees have approved? (If not, insist on waiting until the issue can be discussed at a trustees' meeting.)
- If the payment is for an item with no invoice, such as wages or salaries, is the amount reasonable? (You need to know salary scales of the staff concerned.) Depending on the deductions, salary payments tend to be for awkward amounts, but from time to time you should ask to check the Pay As You Earn (PAYE) calculations. If there are two payments, one to the employee and one to HM Revenue & Customs (HMRC), look at the total of the two. If a salary payment is increased because of overtime or a pay rise, make sure you see the paperwork.
- Before signing for standing orders or direct debits, be sure that the trustees have agreed the relevant payment on an ongoing basis. With

direct debits, where your supplier can vary the charge, is there a proper procedure to check that the amounts going through the bank are correct?

- With cheques to draw petty cash, always insist on seeing the petty cash records explaining how the previous petty cash was spent. Be very suspicious if someone tells you that extra large amounts of petty cash are needed – what are the reasons, and how will the cash be controlled?

- Even if the expenditure looks reasonable in principle, does it fall within agreed budgets (see chapter 9)?

- Even if the expenditure is apparently reasonable, is it appropriate for the fund concerned? For example, an older people's project might have a budget for 'equipment' but if you are asked to sign cheques for children's play equipment, you might be suspicious. (Bills should always be marked to show where the cost will be allocated before anyone is asked to authorise payment.)

- Have you already signed a cheque for the same item? This could be an oversight, but some frauds rely on making payments twice and then diverting the second payment. If there are several co-signatories this needs care – you may want to look back through the cheque book (and with a new cheque book, make sure the cheque numbers run on from the previous one).

However, charities need to take care on payments of all kinds – there is no point in having thorough checks on the payment of small bills unless your controls are just as strict for paying salaries. Since many charities pay salaries by direct bank transfer (BACS) the key issue is who is allowed to sign the transfer mandate? In many charities this is the largest single area of expenditure each month so, ideally, two trustees should sign it (following careful checks of the PAYE calculations). If this is impossible for timing reasons, and the trustees decide to delegate this to a single trustee, the bank should be given an upper limit. Where a member of staff is basically responsible for his or her own salary computations, regular checks are vital. If, as treasurer, you do not really understand PAYE and you leave it to a member of staff, the trustees are taking great risks.

Urgent small payments

Where small payments have to be made urgently, petty cash is one solution. An alternative is to open a small bank account, topped up from time to time by transfers from the main account, where cheques up to a small amount can be signed by just one member of staff. The chief control with such an account will be when making transfers from the main account, on the same lines as when drawing petty cash.

Alternatively, the charity may be eligible for a business credit or debit card in the charity's name. Relevant trustees or members of staff are given individual cards linked to a common account to pay for small items of expenditure agreed in principle by the trustees. But the limits on such cards must be very modest (perhaps no more than £250 a month) and the statements need to be checked carefully each month by someone *other* than the cardholders, with a clear procedure for alerting trustees if unauthorised expenditure appears. Many charities have been victims of serious frauds by treasurers or staff running up personal expenditure on such cards that have remained unchecked for too long. If the treasurer is the person who checks the card statements then he or she should *not* have a card. Also, the issue of any additional cards should always require two signatures.

Purchases and expenditure commitments

Expenditure should not only be controlled at the stage of writing the cheque. If something has been bought, and the charity has received an invoice from the supplier, it is hard for trustees to refuse to sign a cheque at that stage. So, care is needed to ensure that members of staff cannot commit the charity to expenditure of any kind unless the trustees have approved it (either in terms of an overall budget for an activity or, with large items, on a one-off basis). Similarly, any new contracts of employment or notification of pay rises to existing staff should require formal trustee approval. If there is clear written guidance on these lines, you would have the possible sanction of disciplinary action if a member of staff deliberately incurred expenditure outside such rules.

Control of income

Many charities have fairly strict controls on expenditure but are quite lax on the income side. There are two main risks to consider:

- the risk of income due to the charity being diverted;
- the risk of accepting income where the obligations are too great in relation to the amount received, so that the net effect is a drain on the charity's funds.

On the first point, charities are particularly vulnerable, especially in terms of donations. A customer who sent a payment to a business but did not receive the items ordered would almost certainly complain, but a donor who hears nothing in response to their donation may simply assume the charity is saving administrative costs by not issuing receipts. A donor who puts money into a cash collection certainly does not expect a receipt. So trustees need to establish systems to reduce the chances of income going astray.

On the second point, it is vital that trustees are involved in approval of all major funding bids – most funders require a trustee's signature on grant applications, but this is not universal. When it comes to tendering for contracts, there is always a risk, if controls are not in place, that a well-meaning member of staff might submit a tender to carry out work at too low a price. Sometimes the first that the trustees hear about such a contract is when they learn of a new 'successful' funding bid which, when examined, is actually committing the charity to significant new expenditure which the trustees have never agreed. This relates to the key issue of *full cost recovery* (see page 48). If a charity is agreeing to undertake new or additional work and sets too low a price, the net result can be as bad as if incoming donations were being put on a bonfire.

So, whilst the controls in relation to income are very different from expenditure controls, they are just as important.

For charities whose income consists of a small number of large grants, then as long as the trustees approved the grant applications, the main issue is controlling expenditure. But in charities where much of the income comes from ad hoc donations, there is a huge risk of funds being lost because of donations not being banked into the charity's bank account in the first place.

The risk is greatest with incoming cash. If you have cash collections, for example collections at religious services or community events, try to ensure that the money is within sight of at least two independent people from the moment it is given, until it is counted and signed for. You need some kind of record form, signed by both people at the time the cash is counted. With other kinds of collections – in the street or with static boxes – it is best to use collecting boxes with a seal, and have a clear rule that there must be two people present when the seal is removed and the box opened.

Even incoming cheques present risks. If the charity's name is often abbreviated to initials, it is not that difficult for someone dishonest to alter the payee and pay the cheque into a personal account. More serious cases of fraud have involved dishonest treasurers opening an additional bank account in the charity's name, not known to the other trustees or the auditor, and diverting substantial funds through that account.

Many charities that receive ad hoc donations thus try to arrange for all incoming post to be opened with two people present. This can be difficult in a very small organisation, but if you can only manage one person, try to vary the person, have a strict rule on recording all donations as soon as the post is opened, and make regular spot checks.

Control of income is also about making sure that the charity receives all the income promised. If you have donors or funders making promises of future support, you need a system to check that what is received corresponds (at least) to what was promised – some organisations are very lax about sending reminders. With anyone making a regular gift, it is always worth enquiring if the gifts suddenly stop – the person may still wish to give and it could just be an error by their bank. With funding from trusts or public sector grants, where grants are paid in instalments, the charity normally has to complete a monitoring or claim form to receive the second and subsequent instalments: amazingly, some charities fail to make these claims.

Honesty

Clearly no system of checks can be absolutely secure, particularly in a small organisation, and the first point of control is to ensure that all trustees and all staff involved with the finances of the charity are honest and dependable. With staff, taking up references is important. Similarly, if someone relatively new to an organisation volunteers to become treasurer, it is worth enquiring about the person's background, and perhaps seeking a reference from any previous charity with which he or she been involved. Many charities routinely undertake Criminal Record Bureau (CRB) checks on all new trustees. However, this is not an absolute requirement unless the charity is working with children or vulnerable adults, and some charities may not be permitted to undertake such checks. In any case, such checks are of no use unless the trustees have a clear policy as to how the results will be considered.

In many organisations honesty is taken for granted, and sometimes treasurers feel threatened if they are asked to have a witness when counting cash or when the second signatory asks questions before signing a cheque. There is an assumption in much of the voluntary sector that honesty is so fundamental to the organisation's beliefs that independent checks are unnecessary.

However, as many organisations know to their cost, even those with the most noble aims are sometimes led astray. Quite apart from the risk of fraud, a second person looking at cheques and receipts reduces the risk of error. Also, even the most honest treasurers sometimes get months behind with their books if no one asks to see them: the charity as a whole needs a means of picking up signs when a treasurer is no longer coping and needs to step down.

Verifying the books

Having proper controls on income and expenditure is the first step, but you then need to be sure that what is recorded in the books corresponds to what has been agreed. Even the most honest person will make occasional errors, and you need the means to identify these and correct them. There have been cases where, either through fraud or incompetence, the books completely fail to reflect the actual monies coming in and out.

Bank reconciliation

One of the most important checks is to do a bank reconciliation every time a bank statement is received. Whilst this does not prove that everything in the books is correct, it does give a strong confirmation that what has been posted to the bank account in the books of the charity corresponds to what has physically gone through the bank. If you have several bank accounts, you need to do this for each account, and you need to ensure bank statements are received frequently enough so that if there is a discrepancy, you have a reasonable chance of finding the cause (normally you will want a monthly statement on your main current account).

Of course, bank reconciliation is only possible if you are maintaining a bank balance in your books that can be cross checked. Your own figure could be in a 'bank' column in an analysed cashbook (see chapter 5), or in a separate bank ledger (for example in a computer system) or, in a very small organisation, the running bank balance could be maintained as a running cheque book balance (provided you also have a cashbook to analyse the purpose of each receipt or payment).

In general, the bank balance in the books will not correspond to the balance on the bank statement because of the issue of uncleared cheques (also known as 'unpresented' cheques). For example, suppose you wrote a cheque for £50 to Jane Smith on 15 January. If she had not paid it into her own account by about 28 January, it will not appear on your bank statement dated 31 January. In your books, you would have deducted the payment on

15 January, when you wrote the cheque, but at 31 January the money is still in the charity's bank account. If this were the only case, the balance on the bank statement would thus be £50 higher than the balance in your books.

The same problem can also apply with receipts if they were paid in just before the statement date.

In order to allow for uncleared items, you need a means of marking in your books when each cheque, receipt, or any other bank transaction has cleared – many people put a tick against the cheque in their books and on the statement (and computer-based accounting systems often have a means to do this automatically).

You then need to go through the books, noting all uncleared items (which could be in any fund which uses the bank account concerned). Add up the uncleared cheques, and the uncleared receipts if you have any. Remember to include items still uncleared from previous months – in some cases this may mean going back to the previous year's accounts. You can then set down a bank reconciliation calculation (see figure 6.1).

Figure 6.1   Bank reconciliation

Bank reconciliation – Current account as at 31 January

BALANCE OF ACCOUNT AS ON BANK STATEMENT:			£2236.75
Less uncleared cheques:			
	000274	15.00	
	000276	678.00	
		693.00	−693.00
Plus uncleared receipts:	None		+0.00
Expected balance in books:			£1543.75
ACTUAL BALANCE OF BANK ACCOUNT IN BOOKS:			£1543.75

If the bank statement does not end on the exact date at which you are closing the books, be sure to draw a line on the statement at the relevant date, and use that balance (i.e. not the final balance on the statement).

If the expected balance from the calculation ties up with the actual balance recorded in your books, this is a good confirmation of your bookkeeping. If there is a discrepancy, work out the difference between the two figures, and look for an error of that amount.

The possible causes of bank reconciliation errors must always come down to one or more of the following:

- a payment or receipt entered in the books is marked as cleared, but in fact it has *not* yet gone through the bank;
- a payment or receipt is marked in the books as *not* cleared when in fact it *has* appeared on a bank statement;
- an item on the bank statement has not been entered in the books at all (look especially at interest payments, direct debits, bank charges, transfers between accounts, incoming standing orders);
- an item has been entered in the books *twice* (and possibly both entries have been marked as cleared when in fact there was only one item on the bank statement);
- an item was entered in the books as a payment but it was actually a receipt (or vice versa) – if so, the discrepancy on reconciliation will be twice the amount of the item (watch too for transfers between current and deposit accounts which have been posted the wrong way round – this has the same effect);
- an item appears in the books and on the bank statement, but the amounts are different, usually due to a clerical error (this takes a lot of time to spot – get someone to call out the statement while you check the books, or vice versa: note that if the discrepancy divides exactly by nine it is likely to be a transposition error, e.g. a cheque was written for £23.70 but posted in the books as £27.30: the difference is £3.60, which divides by nine);
- if you have several bank accounts, an item has been posted in the books to the wrong account;
- a calculation error in the running balance in the books if maintained manually.

The hardest problems to resolve are where there are two or more errors combined, e.g. a transposition error *and* an item missing, so the total discrepancy does not divide by nine, neither does it tie up with any particular amount entered. But if the reconciliation was correct the previous month, the problem must be something in the books that has changed since then: this is why it is important to do bank reconciliation regularly. Remember that when you mark the books for items that are now cleared, you will often be marking prior months' entries as well as those for the current month. So, in considering what has changed since the previous month, you may be looking at several months' entries.

Other checks on the books

With petty cash, the main check is to count the physical amount of petty cash regularly, to be sure it corresponds with the expected value in the books. If not, is it a clerical error, or has someone been taking petty cash without authority? If the balance in the cash tin is higher than expected – not unknown in charities – it could be because of people putting donations in the tin. It is best to make some other arrangement for cash donations.

With the accounts for the different categories of income and expenditure, physical checks are rarely possible; the main test is one of reasonableness. This is where budgets help enormously. If a given account is heavily over or under budget, is there a good reason, or is it because receipts or payments have been posted correctly as far as the bank account is concerned, but allocated to the wrong income or expenditure category?

With multiple funds, it is particularly important to be certain that all income and expenses are allocated to the correct fund, otherwise restricted funds (see chapter 3) may be used for the wrong purposes. For example, it is not unusual in a charity with multiple projects to find that someone's salary has been charged to the wrong fund for several months. Regular sample checks of this kind by someone other than the treasurer or bookkeeper can help to pick up problems at an early stage.

Subsidiary groups

Many charities have subsidiary groups that handle their own money on a day to day basis, but which are legally part of the main charity.

It is important to remember that money under the control of such groups is part of the funds for which the charity trustees are responsible, and at year end these figures must be included with the 'main' accounts, in order to produce proper year end accounts for the whole charity. (This is called 'consolidation'.)

Make sure that such groups have reasonable controls to prevent money belonging to the charity from going astray, and ensure that charity money is not being held in personal accounts. If such groups have their own bank account, check that proper procedures are followed for cheque signatories and bank reconciliation. To prevent groups harbouring funds that no one knows about, it is important to have a rule that no bank account can be opened by any group without approval by the trustees.

At year end, you may want to give each subsidiary treasurer a form to return to you – see figure 6.2 for an example. These figures can then be posted into the books of the main charity, treating the group as a separate fund and creating an additional bank account or petty cash account in the charity's books for the amounts held by the group. If there are subsidies from the main charity to the group – line (4) – or proceeds transferred from the group to the main charity – line (7) – then although these are seen as receipts or payments from the perspective of the group, they need to be recorded as inter-fund transfers in the accounts of the charity as a whole, in order to ensure that income or expenditure is not counted twice. Once a group has been operating for more than a year, a crucial but simple check is to be sure that the opening balance of the second year agrees with the closing balance from the previous year.

Figure 6.2 Form for subsidiary groups to submit to the overall treasurer

NAME OF CHARITY

Name of group: ....

Year ending: 31 March ....

(1)	Balance of group at 1 April last year: (Cash in hand + bank if applicable)	£....................
(2)	Receipts from group members:	£....................
(3)	Receipts from external sources:	£.................... (give details)
(4)	Contributions from the main charity:	£....................
(5)	Total receipts	£.................... (2)+(3)+(4)
(6)	Payments by group:	£....................
(7)	Proceeds transferred to main charity:	£....................
(8)	Total payments:	£.................... (6)+(7)
(9)	Balance in hand at year end 31 March: (Cash in hand + bank if applicable)	£....................
(10)	Check calculation:	£.................... (1)+(5)–(8)

If lines (9) and (10) are not equal there is an error in your books – please explain.

I confirm that records have been kept of the above items, which can be made available to the charity's auditor or independent examiner on request.

Signed .... *(Group leader)*

7 Final accounts

For many treasurers and finance officers, producing the year end accounts is the most demanding task of the year. But, although you will probably be quite busy in the weeks immediately after year end, if you have been keeping books in good form and maintaining adequate controls, the year end process can be quite rewarding, as you see your work come to fruition and put into a form for digestion by the outside world.

Obviously the work will be considerably less if your books are structured in a way that links closely to the year end accounts. If you are using a computerised accounting system set up in a way that enables you to generate reports in line with the Regulations and Statement of Recommended Practice (SORP), the task is simpler still. (But bear in mind that all transactions for the year, including special entries such as inter-fund transfers, must have been be posted correctly on your system if you want to rely on reports from the system as a basis for your year end accounts.)

Who are the accounts for?

Although several chapters of this book are concerned with the legal requirements for the accounts, it is important to remember that your final accounts are much more than a document to meet charity law.

Companies in business sometimes produce the briefest possible accounts that comply with the law, in order to avoid disclosing too much to their competitors. But for a charity, the opposite usually applies: your annual accounts are a key means of communication with members, funders and supporters (present and future), and you will often want to include more than the legal minimum. Your accounts may also go to umbrella bodies to which you are affiliated, to HM Revenue & Customs (HMRC), Companies House (if your organisation is a charitable company) and elsewhere. If you are applying for grants, your prospective funders may read your accounts much more closely than the Charity Commission or the Office of the Scottish Charity Regulator (OSCR). However, you also want to avoid giving so much detail that readers cannot see the overall picture. To a large extent the legal requirements help in this, by requiring a certain degree of standardisation in the accounts of all charities.

Before preparing a set of accounts for the first time, or before making a major change to the current format, it is worth thinking carefully about all the audiences at whom you are aiming. In principle you could produce different sorts of accounts for different audiences. For example, some larger charities produce full accounts for the Charity Commission and for supporters who want the full detail, and summarised accounts for others. However, for a smaller charity, this is a lot of extra work; the summarised accounts must make clear that they are only a summary, and must include a statement by your auditor or independent examiner that they are not inconsistent with the full accounts. Most local charities find that those supporters who want accounts want the full detail, and others are not really interested in accounts at all.

Similarly, a charitable company in England and Wales could in theory produce one set of accounts complying with the SORP to send to the Charity Commission, and another set complying with the Companies Acts to send to Companies House. But in practice, it is much less work to produce one set of accounts that meets the requirements of both charity law and company law.

What about the annual report?

In law, a charity must produce two public documents at year end – the *annual report* and the *annual accounts*. Each must be approved and signed by the trustees before they can be circulated, and in most cases the accounts must have an auditor's or independent examiner's report (see chapter 8). They can be printed or copied separately, but anyone requesting the accounts must also be given the annual report and vice versa, so it is usually best to combine them into one document called the 'annual report and accounts'.

It is not possible in this book to cover the full requirements for annual reports, but table 7.1 gives a summary of the rules. It may fall to you as treasurer to ensure that the other trustees are aware of these requirements.

Table 7.1   Charity annual reports – summary of requirements

Factual section

(a) Official name of the charity (and any working names)
(b) Registered charity number (if registered) and company number (if applicable)
(c) Official address of the charity*
(d) Particulars of governing document (including date of last amendment)
(e) Description of the objects of the charity (usually this is easily obtained from the constitution or other governing document)
(f) Names* of the charity trustees *as at the date of approving the report*
(g) Names* of all other trustees who served for any part of the financial year
(h) Any external persons* or bodies entitled to appoint trustees to the charity
(i) Names* of holding trustees at date of approval
(j) Any other holding trustees* during year

*If disclosing trustees' names or an official address would put anyone in personal danger, the charity can apply to Charity Commission for permission to omit them.

Narrative section (public benefit report)

- Statement that the trustees have considered Charity Commission guidance on public benefit
- Charities below the audit threshold:[1] a brief review of the main activities undertaken during the year in terms of public benefit achieved
- Charities over the audit threshold:[1] review of significant activities undertaken during the year in terms of public benefit achieved – including the trustees' aims for the year, progress against the aims, contribution of volunteers and principal funding sources

Policies section

- Policy on level of reserves
- Action being taken on any funds in deficit

Extras needed for charities over the audit threshold[1]

- Organisational structure
- Risk assessment
- Policy on trustee induction and training
- Investment policy and review of investment performance
- Grant-making policy

Approval

This report was approved by the trustees on [date] and is signed on their behalf by . . . . [normally two trustees should sign].

[1]The audit threshold is currently £500,000 income or £3.26 million assets – see chapter 2 for further details.

This table gives a summary of the rules in England and Wales – for full details see Regulation 40 of Charities (Accounts and Reports) Regulations 2008. The rules for charities registered in Scotland are very similar – see Schedule 2 of the Charities Accounts (Scotland) Regulations 2006 if the accounts are on a receipts and payments basis. With fully accrued accounts, Scottish charities simply need to follow the annual report requirements in SORP 2005, which – in summary – are as above.

The most important part of the annual report is the narrative section, which explains what the charity has actually done during the year. The Charities (Accounts and Reports) Regulations 2008 (which implement changes under the Charities Act 2006) place further emphasis on this by requiring trustees to highlight how the charity has 'furthered its purposes for the benefit of the public'. In other words, the work of the charity must be explained in terms of how it has advanced its objects and the public benefit requirement – see *What is a charity* in chapter 1 (page 5) for more on this. So, for example, the annual report should not just contain reports on fundraising events or thanks to individuals; the focus should be on what the charity has done to advance its objects and how people have benefited.

The link between the annual report and the annual accounts is absolutely crucial in enabling someone who does not understand the charity to get a proper understanding (SORP 2005 refers to this on many occasions). Quite often there will be cross-references between them; for example, the accounts of a grant-making charity may include a note that refers readers to the annual report for the full list of grants made. A service-providing charity may describe each project in the annual report (explaining which projects are managed as separate funds) and then refer readers to the particular note in the accounts with figures for each fund (see figure 9.2 on page 125 for an example of a report which could well be used for such a note).

The treasurer is usually responsible for arranging the preparation of the annual accounts, but it may be that someone else in the charity – perhaps the secretary or chief officer – will draft the annual report. However, in such cases there needs to be a good deal of liaison, especially if there are cross-references. Liaison is particularly crucial on aspects of the annual report dealing with financial issues, such as comments on funding, the financial performance for the year, the statement of the reserves policy (see chapter 4) and any comments on funds in deficit.

In the case of a charitable company, it is usual to provide one report that is both the directors' annual report required under company law and the trustees' annual report required under charity law. This dual requirement is sometimes overlooked: a report that only covers the requirements of the Companies Acts is certainly not sufficient. Furthermore, a report that fails to give a proper review of the charity's activities can be disastrous when applying for funding.

The annual report must be a report by the trustees as a whole, and signed on their behalf. Some charities like to produce an attractive document with reports by key individuals, comments by participants or users, photographs and much more. With care on the wording, this can be incorporated into the legal annual report, so long as the whole document is approved and signed by the trustees.

However, if you want to produce an unofficial publication about the work of the charity, it is best to issue this as a completely separate document, and call it an *annual review* (or something similar) to make it clear that it is not the legal annual report. Tell people in such a document how they can obtain the annual report and accounts if they want a copy. (It is generally best to avoid giving figures in an annual review, or they may amount to summary accounts, and hence need a statement by your auditor or examiner, as explained above.)

Who prepares the accounts?

The term 'preparing the accounts' means taking the information from the books and turning them into a final document which, once approved and signed by the trustees, can be copied and circulated. Nowadays the document is almost always created electronically, so a draft can easily be amended (but in principle, for a very small charity, the document could still be handwritten or typewritten).

Except in the very smallest organisations, your accounts will then be subject to audit or independent examination (see chapter 8). So it is usual to involve your auditor or examiner while the accounts are still in draft. Depending on their complexity and the relative experience in preparing accounts, there are four main ways of sharing the work.

1   *Auditor/examiner appointed only to report*
    In this 'pure audit' model, the charity produces final accounts complying with the regulations, etc.; these accounts are approved and signed by trustees. They are then submitted to the auditor/examiner for scrutiny and report.

2   *Auditor/examiner may request amendments and then reports*
    In this approach, the charity produces draft final accounts, including the full notes. These are submitted to the auditor/examiner for provisional approval or to request amendment. The amendments are then incorporated and the accounts signed by the trustees. The auditor/examiner then attaches and signs his or her report.

3   *Auditor/examiner completes accounts and then reports*
    The charity produces the basis of the accounts – perhaps the main financial reports from an accounting system and a summary of items

for the notes. The auditor/examiner then turns these into a full set of accounts. These (externally finalised) accounts are presented to the charity and signed by the trustees, and the auditor/examiner then signs his or her report.

4 *Auditor/examiner produces accounts from scratch and reports on them*
   In charities with very limited financial experience, it often happens that the charity provides the auditor/examiner purely with the books. From these, the auditor/examiner prepares a full set of accounts from scratch. These (externally prepared) accounts are signed by the trustees and the auditor/examiner then signs his or her report.

Which approach to use?

If possible, approaches 2 or 3 are best. These allow a proper dialogue between the charity and the auditor or examiner. The main difference between them is that in approach 2 the charity does the word processing of the final document and the auditor/examiner requests changes; in approach 3 it is the other way round.

Although approach 1 can work with very small organisations, the problem is that if the auditor/examiner is unhappy with anything in the accounts, there is no alternative but to issue a qualified report (i.e. an audit or examination report that contains qualifications or reservations). It can be quite damaging to the charity to have to circulate accounts with a qualified auditor's/examiner's report. If a small amendment to the accounts – perhaps adding an extra note – would have solved the problem, it is much better to be able to incorporate this before final approval by the trustees.

The main problem with approach 4 is that if someone outside the charity does almost everything, will your trustees be able to make a sensible decision about approving the accounts? Remember that in law, producing the accounts is the responsibility of the charity trustees. It is fine for the trustees to use an accountant to *help* prepare the accounts, but the trustees are responsible for the content.

For example, if the books did not properly distinguish a restricted fund (because the bookkeeper included a special grant with general donations) there is no way that an accountant could know this unless they are told. If accounts are prepared showing money in the general fund that should be restricted, it is up to the trustees to spot this when considering approval of the accounts, and ask for the draft to be changed before they sign.

Many charities get into the circular argument of saying 'these accounts have been prepared by our accountants so they must be correct'. Then the accountant (now acting as auditor/examiner) says 'since the accounts were based on the books which I saw and since they have been approved by the trustees, the content must be OK' and each is signing on the basis of an assumption of what the other has done.

The content of the final accounts

As explained in chapter 2, there are two possible formats for the final accounts:

- receipts and payments accounts; or
- accruals accounts, which have to comply with the SORP.

Note that these are the only formats permitted by law in England, Wales and Scotland (and similar principles will soon apply in Northern Ireland). Mixtures of receipts and payments and accruals, and other formats from the past, will not generally meet the needs of charity law.

The rest of this chapter explains the general framework. But preparing final accounts, particularly accruals accounts in SORP format, involves much more than can be covered in a book of this length. There are plenty of books giving more detailed advice – see *Further reading*. Figures 7.2 and 7.4 illustrate the formats you will commonly see (but beware of using these examples as models, because different information may be needed in different charities).

Final receipts and payments accounts

The Charities Act 1993 says that when a charity opts to produce receipts and payments accounts, the trustees must provide:

- a receipts and payments account (which must distinguish the different funds of the charity); and
- a statement of assets and liabilities (SOAL).

This also applies for receipts and payments accounts under the Charities Act (Northern Ireland) 2008. In Scotland, the SOAL is replaced by a 'statement of balances' but the idea is very similar; however the Scottish regulations are more specific on the different categories needed for receipts and payments.

Figure 7.2   Example receipts and payments accounts

MIDSHAM COMMUNITY ASSOCIATION - ACCOUNTS FOR TH■

GENERAL FUND: RECEIPTS AND PAYMENTS (Unrestricted Fund)

2010/11		2011/12
£		£
	Receipts	
467	Members' Subscriptions	534
10000	Council Grant	25000
500	Miscellaneous Donations	429
0	Tax Reclaimed on Gift Aid	140
1103	Christmas Bazaar	1732
71	Bank Interest	53
12141	TOTAL RECEIPTS	27888
	Payments	
980	Administrator Salary	1079
934	Heat and Light	869
389	Rates, Water Rates, Cleaning	403
6981	Repairs and Maintenance	3708
321	Stationery	291
783	Publicity Literature	1781
1089	Postage and Telephone	1237
0	Purchase of Minibus	18000
200	Independent Examiner's Fee	200
171	Committee Travel Expenses	126
0	Contribution to Outreach Project	100
11848	TOTAL PAYMENTS	27794
293	SURPLUS	94
80	Balance brought forward 01 Apr 11	373
373	Balance carried forward 31 Mar 12	467

OUTREACH FUND: RECEIPTS AND PAYMENTS (Restricted Fund)

2010/11		2011/12
£		£
	Receipts	
0	Grant from Midsham Trust	4000
0	Participants' Activity Fees	713
0	Contribution from General Fund	100
0	TOTAL RECEIPTS	4813
	Payments	
0	Outreach Worker Wages	2760
0	Outreach Travel Costs	452
0	Outreach Activities	1342
0	TOTAL PAYMENTS	4554
0	SURPLUS	259
0	Balance brought forward 01 Apr 11	0
0	Balance carried forward 31 Mar 12	259

YEAR ENDING 31 MARCH 2012 (Receipts and Payments Format)

STATEMENT OF ASSETS AND LIABILITIES AT 31 MAR 2012

31 Mar 11 £		31 Mar 12 £
	Monetary Assets	
	Current Asset Investments	
250	Investment Account – Midwest Bank	690
	Cash at Bank and in Hand	
115	Current Account – Midwest Bank	21
8	Petty Cash	15
123	Total Cash at Bank and in Hand	36
373	TOTAL MONETARY ASSETS	726
	Represented by Funds	
	Unrestricted Funds	
373	General Fund	467
	Restricted Funds	
0	Outreach Project	259
373	TOTAL FUNDS	726
	Non-Monetary Assets and Liabilities	
	Fixed Assets for Charity Use	
120000	Community Centre	120000
0	Minibus	18000
2000	Furniture and Equipment	1800
122000	Total Fixed Assets for Charity Use	139800
	Debtors	
140	Tax due from HM Revenue & Customs	170
	Creditors Due Within One Year	
−200	Independent Examination Fee Due	−250
121940	TOTAL NON-MONETARY ASSETS	139720

These accounts were approved by the Trustees on 24 May 2012 and signed on their behalf by:

K PATEL – Chairperson
J CORRIGAN – Treasurer

NOTES TO THE ACCOUNTS

1. These accounts are prepared on a receipts and payments basis, with all revenue and expenses shown on a cash basis. Non-monetary assets and liabilities are shown at estimates of the value at the end of the year.
2. The charity has two funds: an unrestricted General Fund and an Outreach Project. The latter is a restricted fund supported mainly by a grant from the Midsham Trust, enabling the charity to employ a P/T outreach worker to visit families in two particular wards with high levels of disadvantage. As a condition of the funding application, the charity itself provided £100 towards this project: this is shown as a transfer from General Fund to the Outreach Fund.
3. All bank interest is allocated to the General Fund.
4. No remuneration was paid to any trustee. Travel expenses totalling £176 were paid to four trustees: £126 of this was from the General Fund, and £50 from the Outreach Project Fund.

Receipts and payments accounts

In England and Wales, and in Northern Ireland, there are no rules in law about how the receipts and payments account is to be laid out, so you are free to break down the receipts and payments into whatever categories you feel would be helpful to your readers. However, the Charity Commission publishes some very helpful guidance (and there were also some helpful sections in the 2000 SORP regarding receipts and payments accounts, but these were not continued in SORP 2005). It is normal to include a comparative column for the previous year, which means trying to keep the same categories from year to year.

Where there are several funds, you can show a completely separate receipts and payments account for each fund (if so, it is more readable if you use a separate page for each fund). But if there are more than about three funds, and particularly if there have been transfers between funds, it may be clearer to show all funds together in a SOFA-type layout (see figure 7.4), so long as it is clearly labelled as being on a 'receipts and payments basis'. However, if several funds are added together into one column, a note explaining the different funds is clearly needed.

Statement of assets and liabilities (SOAL)

The SOAL must list all the assets and liabilities of the charity. It is easiest to divide this into the monetary assets (which will correspond to the balances of funds) and other, non-monetary assets and liabilities such as fixed assets, debtors and creditors. In principle the non-monetary assets could be presented as just a list of items, but if you have estimates of values it is sensible to show them.

Hopefully, as treasurer you will know about any unpaid bills and amounts due to the charity and will thus be able to work out the debtors and creditors, and you will know about new capital items bought during the year. But the fixed assets must include all long-term items owned by the charity (including items acquired or given many years previously), and if no one has produced one before, you may have to compile a fixed asset list from scratch. Do not forget to include buildings and investments, as well as obvious items of furniture, equipment and vehicles. Also, make sure you know about any loans or other commitments: these will need to appear as liabilities on the SOAL.

From this it is clear that, even with receipts and payments accounting, the task of the treasurer is more than just keeping track of the money: you must know about fixed assets, debtors and creditors even if these do not actually appear in the day to day books. But once you have produced the SOAL for one year, you can produce it quite easily in future years by altering each value for the relevant non-monetary items.

Notes to the accounts

With receipts and payments accounts, in England, Wales and Northern Ireland there is no legal requirement to show notes to the accounts. However, in practice your accounts will be much more meaningful to readers if you include relevant information by way of notes – certainly the Charity Commission's guidance is that the accounts should make clear which funds are restricted and should give details of any payments to trustees (including expenses). Table 7.3 lists the notes needed for receipts and payments accounts in Scotland, but charities throughout the UK would be well advised to follow this list (cross-references to the annual report are permitted if relevant details have been given there).

Table 7.3 List of notes for receipts and payments accounts

(a) The nature and purpose of each fund, including details of restrictions on specific funds.

(b) Details of grants paid (number, amounts, types of activities supported, and whether the grants were to organisations or to individuals).

(c) Details of any remuneration or fees paid to any trustees or their close relatives or businesses (a nil statement is needed even if there were no such payments).

(d) Total expenses paid to trustees, including the number of trustees involved (or a nil statement if applicable – e.g. 'No expenses were paid to any of the trustees during the year').

(e) Other information needed to assist readers to understand the accounts.

(Summarised from Schedule 3 Part 2 of the Charities Accounts (Scotland) Regulations 2006.)

Final accruals accounts

Once you move on to accruals accounts, the figures will be slightly different because debtors, creditors and fixed assets are included in the fund balances. (Generally this is compulsory for charities with more than £250,000 income in England and Wales or £100,000 in Scotland or Northern Ireland, but see chapter 2 for details and dates of changes.) Furthermore, accruals accounts must be presented in accordance with the Regulations, which means using 'SORP format'. So the accounts will consist of:

- a statement of financial activities (SOFA)
- a balance sheet
- notes to the accounts.

The rules are quite specific about the principles and layout of the SOFA and balance sheet, and on information that must be given in the notes to the accounts. There are some minor concessions for charities with income of £500,000 or below, but in general once a charity issues accruals accounts, the full SORP presentation must be used.

Figure 7.4   Example accruals accounts

MIDSHAM COMMUNITY ASSOCIATION - ACCOUNTS FOR THE

STATEMENT OF FINANCIAL ACTIVITIES I APRIL 2011 TO 31 MARCH 2012

	2011/2012				2010/11
	Unrestricted Funds £	Restricted Funds £	Capital Funds £	Total Funds £	All Funds £
Incoming Resources					
Generated Funds:					
Voluntary Income	25599	4000		29599	*10500*
Sales from Fundraising Activities	1732			1732	*1103*
Investment Income	53			53	*71*
Charitable Activities:					
Subscriptions and Fees	534	713		1247	*467*
Total Incoming Resources	27918	4713	0	32631	*12141*
Resources Expended					
Costs of Generating Funds:					
Fundraising for Voluntary Income	1781			1781	*783*
Cost of Goods Sold	281			281	*321*
Investment Management Costs	10			10	*0*
Charitable Activities:					
Community Services	12246	4504		16750	*10573*
Governance Costs:	126	50		176	*171*
Total Resources Used	14444	4554	0	18998	*11848*
NET RESOURCES BEFORE TRANSFERS	13474	159	0	13633	*293*
Transfers Between Funds					
Contribution to Project	−100	100		0	*0*
NET MOVEMENT IN FUNDS	13374	259	0	13633	*293*
Fund Balances Brought Forward 01 Apr 11	2313	0	120000	122313	*122020*
Fund Balances Carried Forward 31 Mar 12	15687	259	120000	135946	*122313*

The notes on page 3 to 6 form part of these accounts.

NOTES TO THE ACCOUNTS

This example does not show the notes – however, as these are accruals accounts, full notes covering all the issues required by the Regulations and SORP will be needed on the pages after the Balance Sheet. In a simple charity such as this, the notes might include:

1. Accounting policies.
2. Description of each fund and explanation of inter-fund transfers.
3. Summary of movements on each fund (this would be needed if more than one fund was included in any column of the SOFA) – [see example on page 125]
4. Breakdown of the expenditure on charitable activities.
5. Table of fixed asset movements showing additions, depreciation etc, for each type of assets.
6. Explanation of debtors (unless fully shown on balance sheet).
7. Explanation of creditors (unless fully shown on balance sheet).
8. Details of staff numbers and salary costs.
9. Explanation of trustees expenses, and a statement that there were no other transactions with trustees.
10. Note of independent examiner's fee.
11. Details of any grants made to other organisations (or individuals).
12. A breakdown of the net assets across the unrestricted, restricted and capital funds.

The notes also need to include last year's comparisons where applicable.

YEAR ENDING 31 MARCH 2012 (Accruals Basis – SORP Format)

BALANCE SHEET AT 31 MARCH 2012

	31 March 12 £	31 Mar 11 £
Assets and Liabilities		
FIXED ASSETS		
Tangible Fixed Assets		
Community Centre	120000	120000
Minibus	13500	0
Furniture and Equipment	1800	2000
Total Fixed Assets for Charity Use	135300	122000
CURRENT ASSETS		
Debtors		
Tax due from HM Revenue & Customs	170	140
Current Asset Investments		
30 Day Account Midwest Bank	690	250
Cash at Bank and in Hand		
Current Account – Midwest Bank	21	115
Petty Cash	15	8
Total Cash at Bank and in Hand	36	123
	896	513
CURRENT LIABILITIES		
Creditors Due Within One Year		
Independent Examination Fee Due	−250	−200
NET CURRENT ASSETS	646	313
TOTAL ASSETS LESS CURRENT LIABILITIES	135946	122313
NET ASSETS	135946	122313
Represented by Funds		
Unrestricted Funds		
General Fund	15687	2313
Restricted Funds		
Outreach Project	259	0
Capital Funds		
Buildings Reserve	120000	120000
TOTAL FUNDS	135946	122313

Approved by the Trustees on 24 May 2012 and signed on their behalf by:

K PATEL – Chairperson
J CORRIGAN – Treasurer

NOTES TO THE ACCOUNTS
(These will follow on subsequent pages – see box opposite.)

Statement of financial activities (SOFA)

The SOFA is essentially an income and expenditure account divided into columns for the three types of funds: unrestricted funds (this includes designated funds); restricted income funds; and capital or endowment funds (see chapter 3 for definitions). There is also a column showing the total income and expenditure of all funds, and a comparison column with the overall totals for the last year.

The SOFA can seem complex at first, but once people get used to it, it can prove to be a very helpful way of understanding the income and expenditure of an organisation, without confusing restricted and unrestricted funds, but showing the whole charity on one page. There is a separate line for any transfers between funds, so support from one fund to another is not confused with external income or expenditure – see chapters 3 and 4 for more on this. This line must, of course, total to zero in the 'All funds' column, because the transfers out of one fund must be balanced by transfers into other funds. Sometimes the SOFA will include a further section for gains and losses where assets are revalued, but this is not shown in the example.

Within each column there may be several funds added together – for example the second column could have the totals for 10 or more projects supported by restricted funds – but notes to the accounts must give individual balances for each fund (see figure 9.2, page 125 for an example).

As well as specifying the columns, the SORP rules specify the general headings to be used for income and expenditure, in order to ensure comparability between different charities. These tend to vary slightly with each revision of the SORP – the format in figure 7.4 is based on SORP 2005.

For full SORP format, the income and expenditure must be broken down on a functional basis, showing how much was spent on particular purposes. So, for example, rather than having a single expenditure line for 'salaries', salary costs for fundraising come under 'Cost of generating funds', time spent on the main work of the charity appears under 'Charitable activities', and if significant staff time has been used, for example, supporting the trustees or organising annual general meetings (AGMs), this can be included in 'Governance costs'. In a medium-sized charity, this may mean splitting the salaries of individual staff.

If this seems too hard, charities below the audit threshold (£500,000 income or £3.26 million assets) are allowed to use natural classifications of expenditure on the SOFA (for example 'Salaries', 'Premises', 'Running costs', 'Depreciation') to simplify things. Likewise smaller charities can now also use a natural breakdown for the different kinds of income to the charity.

The balance sheet

The balance sheet shows all the charity's assets and liabilities, balanced against the relevant funds. The key thing to appreciate with accruals accounts is that the value of every fixed asset, debtor or creditor is included in the relevant fund (unlike receipts and payments accounts, where the fund balances consist only of money). (See chapter 10 for more on this.)

The top half of the balance sheet is similar to the format used for business accounts, but the bottom half is quite different because all the assets and liabilities belong to the charity. All assets are held either for the general objects of the charity (unrestricted funds), or for certain restricted or capital purposes.

Like the SOFA, the content and layout of the balance sheet is laid down by the Regulations and SORP. One key requirement is that any investments (including property) must be shown at market value (rather than at their original cost).

The balance sheet must be signed by the trustees to show that they have approved the accounts.

Notes to the accounts

Unlike receipts and payments accounts, where (except in Scotland) notes are at the discretion of the charity concerned, with accruals accounts it is a legal requirement to provide a great deal of additional information in notes to the accounts. All the points shown in table 7.5 must be covered by notes, if there is anything applicable.

Whilst an appropriate accounting system can help to produce the SOFA, balance sheet and one or two key notes, most of the task of preparing the notes is best done by word processing. Although the rules state what is required in the notes, the charity is free to choose the wording: if you are using a professional accountant to help prepare the accounts, try to ensure that the notes are worded in a language that will make sense to other

Table 7.5 Accruals accounts – summary of requirements for notes to the accounts

(a) Adjustments to last year's figures
(b) Accounting policies and estimation techniques
(c) Details of any material changes to accounting policies and techniques
(d) Nature and purpose of each fund following SORP principles (normally provide a table with a line for each fund showing opening balance, income, expenditure, transfers and closing balance (see example in figure 9.2, page 125)
(e) Transactions with related parties (i.e. with trustees and their relatives or businesses) including trustees' expenses paid (if none, must say none)
(f) Total staff costs (split into gross salaries, employer's national insurance (NI), and employer's pension contributions)
(g) Details of individual staff salaries over £60,000 (in £10,000 bands) (if none, must say none)
(h) Details of any incoming resources to capital/endowment funds
(i) Details of inter-fund transfers affecting restricted funds, with explanations
(j) Details of any subsidiaries of the charity (including turnover, net profit and details of any audit report)
(k) Details of any guarantees given to third parties
(l) Loans – to the charity (if secured on the charity's property) or loans made by the charity to others
(m) Explanation of any funds in deficit (and in such cases, a note will also be needed in the annual report explaining the trustees' proposed action – see table 7.1)
(n) Auditor's/independent examiner's remuneration (and fees for any other services provided to the charity by the auditor/examiner)
(o) Grants made – details as specified in SORP
(p) Details of any ex gratia payments made
(q) Breakdown of the SOFA resources expended line 'Charitable activities' – first this should be split into the main separate activities of the charity, and then for each activity give:
 • cost of work undertaken directly by the charity itself
 • grant-making activity
 • support costs
(r) Breakdown of support costs (details as in SORP)
(s) Analysis of balance sheet figures for fixed assets, debtors, creditors (details as in SORP)
(t) Analysis of all material movements in fixed asset values – this may be combined with (s) – it is usual to give three separate notes:
 • debtors
 • creditors
 • fixed assets – in categories showing additions, disposals, depreciation, revaluations
(u) Previous year's figures for all the above except (i), (o) and (t)
(v) Accounting standards used (SORP 2005, etc.) and details of any major departures
(w) Reasons for any change of accounting date
(x) Reasons if any departure from the Regulations had to be made in order for the accounts to give a true and fair view
(y) Any other information needed to give a true and fair view or to assist the user to understand the accounts

This is a summary – for full details see Schedule 2 to the Charities (Accounts and Reports Regulations) 2008.

See also the SORP 2005 for several further notes required which are not in the Regulations: for example the SORP also requires a breakdown of net assets between funds, details of grant and contract income, details of fundraising activities and breakdown of governance costs.

readers. You can always give more information than the legal minimum if it will help readers understand what the charity is doing.

It usually takes several pages to cover all these issues, so the shortest SORP-compliant accounts tend to be around five pages: the SOFA, balance sheet and three or more pages of notes.

Specialist software is available to help accountants prepare a full set of accounts in SORP format, including all the notes (and a few larger charities use such software themselves). The better products can be very useful in generating smartly presented final accounts that cover the vast majority of the SORP requirements. However, much of the content – for example explaining the purpose of each fund, or details of grants made – must be drafted individually for each charity: it is not unusual to see such notes missing from charity accounts if they were based on a template from another charity. Even with the best accounts preparation systems, the wording and layout for one charity may not be appropriate for another, so take care to review the draft accounts carefully and ask for notes to be reworded to make them clear to your readers, or to add additional notes if appropriate.

Additional reports

In a few cases, accruals-based charity accounts may need additional financial statements in addition to the SOFA and balance sheet – although these rarely arise for smaller charities.

A charitable company will occasionally need a separate income and expenditure account for the purposes of the Companies Acts. However, this only applies in rare cases (e.g. where a charity has received new capital funds), where company accounting requires a different treatment from the SORP. Apart from such special cases, the 'All funds' column on the SOFA will usually meet the Companies Act requirements.

Very large charities (those with any two of the following: more than £6.5 million income; more than £3.26 million assets; or more than 50 employees) must also include a cashflow statement.

Charities with subsidiaries – group accounts

In cases where a charity owns a subsidiary company, or in a few rare cases where one charity is a subsidiary of another, there may be a legal requirement to prepare 'group accounts' – accounts based on taking the figures from the charity and its subsidiary (or subsidiaries) together. This has long been a recommendation under the SORP, and group accounts are now a legal requirement for many charities in England and Wales as a result of the Charities Act 2006.

Normally, the accounts of a charity with a subsidiary will include a single line on the SOFA under 'Incoming Resources – Generated Funds' for the profits donated to the charity by the subsidiary. But if group accounts are needed, the entire SOFA and balance sheet usually have to be presented in double columns, with figures for the charity itself and for the 'group' (i.e. the charity plus its subsidiaries).

The threshold at which group accounts become compulsory is linked to the audit threshold – it is based on £500,000 'aggregate gross income' across the whole group (i.e. the income of the charity, plus the income of the subsidiaries, but deducting income received by the charity from subsidiaries to prevent double counting). The details of group accounts are beyond the scope of this book, but your auditors should be able to help. If your charity has a subsidiary and has aggregate gross income of more than £500,000, the charity will always need an audit (even though the charity's own income could be well below this). See chapter 8 for more on audits and auditors.

8 Audit and independent examination

As explained in the previous chapter, your trustees are responsible for producing the annual accounts. They may seek help from an accountant or independent examiner to get them correctly presented to meet requirements but that is simply helping the trustees, it is quite different from the task of scrutinising the accounts from an independent perspective.

Except in the very smallest charities, once the accounts are complete there is a further legal requirement before they can be circulated – they must be subjected to independent scrutiny by someone unconnected with the trustees. This person will provide a report, which must be attached to the accounts. Many people use the term 'audit' to describe this process, but this is slightly misleading because, as we will see, only the largest charities need a full audit.

The independent report is a vital protection for all concerned. Most funders and donors expect any organisations that they support to produce independently scrutinised accounts. It is also a vital issue for the trustees themselves, because inevitably the day to day finances have to be delegated. So an independent report on the final accounts enables the trustees to have confidence in the overall position of the charity.

Forms of scrutiny

There are two possible forms of independent scrutiny for the accounts of a charity:

- independent examination
- full audit.

These two kinds of scrutiny now apply through the UK, although the precise duties and thresholds vary slightly between England/Wales, Scotland, and Northern Ireland.

Until recently, there was a further form of scrutiny – by a 'reporting accountant' on the accounts of a charitable company – but now charitable companies below the audit threshold can have an independent examination in the same way as other charities.

It is vital to know which of these is required, and what sort of person you can approach. Many people talk loosely about 'audited accounts', but the

Charities Acts draw a clear distinction between audit and independent examination, so it is worth using the terms correctly.

The rules are largely based on the organisation's total income (nowadays only the current year has to be considered) but there are some differences for charities with more than £2.8 million of assets. There are also some slight differences between England and Wales, Scotland, and Northern Ireland. (As explained in chapter 2, the charity accounting rules in Northern Ireland are enacted but are not expected to take effect before 2011.)

The different levels of requirements for charity accounts are shown in tables 2.3, 2.4 and 2.5, in chapter 2. However, tables 8.1 and 8.2 set out the current minimum requirements in law specifically related to the *scrutiny* of charity accounts.

Table 8.1 Minimum requirements for accounts scrutiny – normal charities with modest assets (not more than £3.26 million)*

MINIMUM PERMITTED SCRUTINY OF ACCOUNTS	CHARITIES IN ENGLAND AND WALES	SCOTTISH CHARITIES (and other charities registered with OSCR wherever based)	CHARITIES IN NORTHERN IRELAND
	Income levels:	Income levels:	Income levels:
Approval of accounts by trustees only	£0 to £25,000	Not permitted	Not permitted
Independent examination by examiner of charity's choice	£25,000 to £250,000	£0 to £100,000 (if receipts and payments accounts)	£0 to £100,000
Independent examination by professionally qualified examiner	£250,000 to £500,000	£100,000 to £500,000 (and below £100,000 if accruals accounts)	£100,000 to £500,000
Full audit	More than £500,000	£500,000 or over	More than £500,000

* This table applies from April 2009 onwards (although the legal requirements for Northern Ireland are not expected to take effect until 2011). See the appendix for a summary of the different thresholds over time. In Scotland the asset limit remains £2.8 million assets until April 2011. The receipts and payments limit in Scotland is set to increase to £250,000 for years starting from April 2011. The level of assets does not affect charities in Northern Ireland.

Table 8.2 Minimum requirements for accounts scrutiny – charities with substantial assets (over £3.26 million)*

MINIMUM PERMITTED SCRUTINY OF ACCOUNTS	CHARITIES IN ENGLAND AND WALES	SCOTTISH CHARITIES (and other charities registered with OSCR wherever based)	CHARITIES IN NORTHERN IRELAND
	Income levels:	Income levels:	Income levels:
Approval of accounts by trustees only	£0 to £25,000	Not permitted	Not permitted
Independent examination by examiner of charity's choice	£25,000 to £250,000	£0 to £100,000 (if receipts and payments accounts)	£0 to £100,000
Independent examination by professionally qualified examiner	Not applicable	£0 to £100,000 (accruals accounts)	£100,000 to £500,000
Full audit	More than £250,000	£100,000 or over	More than £500,000

* See footnote to table 8.1

Some charities may need more scrutiny than the minimum set out in the table. For example, although charities in England and Wales are not required under the Charities Act to have an independent examination if their income is £25,000 or below, an independent examination might still be required, by a funder, or by the rules of any umbrella body to which they belong. Similarly, some charities whose income would normally put them clearly in the independent examination band may have a governing document that requires a full audit.

Approval of accounts by trustees only

In England and Wales, for charities with income of £25,000 or below, generally no independent scrutiny is required, and your trustees can simply approve the accounts themselves. This is intended to keep things simple for many small trusts and local voluntary groups with modest income.

But it is important to appreciate that there must still be a formal trustees' meeting at which the accounts are approved, and the trustees need to consider what this involves. As treasurer, you will probably have prepared the accounts and presented them to the trustees, but should they approve them just on your say? This is unwise, because no matter how much they trust you, something could have gone wrong – what if you have simply mistyped a crucial figure? There should still be at least one other trustee, not involved in the day to day bookkeeping, who goes back to the original records and considers whether the accounts are correct before recommending their approval to the rest of the trustees.

At this level most charities will choose to do receipts and payments accounts, but remember this is not allowed for charitable companies. So even though the accounts will not need external scrutiny, a charitable company with under £25,000 income must produce proper accounts on an accruals basis complying with the Companies Acts and the Charities SORP.

However, this option for the trustees of a small charity to approve the accounts without external scrutiny *only* applies in England and Wales. For charities registered in Scotland or Northern Ireland the accounts must at least have an independent examination no matter how small the income.

Independent examination

Until the Charities Acts 1992 and 1993, many smaller charities had an 'informal audit' whereby someone with modest accounting knowledge was asked to look over the books and sign his or her name at the end of the accounts. But these kind of informal audits were often haphazard, with no indication of what the 'honorary auditor' had actually done. Even with accounts prepared by professional accountants, the accountants' report often said only 'These accounts have been prepared from the books and vouchers presented to us' with no opinion as to their completeness or accuracy.

Independent examination was brought in to replace the 'informal audits' of the past, by providing a scrutiny regime which would give some real certainty without requiring smaller charities to bear the cost of a full audit. In England and Wales, independent examination is now usually appropriate for most charities with income in the range £25,000 to £500,000 (in Scotland and Northern Ireland there is no lower limit – even a charity with £5 income needs an independent examination). The two main differences between independent examination and audit relate to who can act and the nature of the report attached to the accounts.

A wide range of people can potentially be independent examiners, though there are important criteria to consider, as explained below, and in some cases (see tables 8.1 and 8.2) it is a legal requirement to use a professionally qualified independent examiner. But the task of an independent examiner is much more than just looking at the accounts to check the figures. In England and Wales the duties are laid down by section 43 of the Charities Act 1993, by Regulation 12 of the Charities (Accounts and Reports) Regulations 2008, and by the Directions of the Charity Commission on the Carrying Out of an Independent Examination. Slightly different rules apply in Scotland under the Charities Accounts (Scotland) Regulations 2006, but the principles are similar. Directions similar to those in England and Wales are likely to be issued by the Charity Commission for Northern Ireland. For Scotland, OSCR has published guidance for independent examiners which is very helpful if not legally binding. No one can validly claim to have carried out an independent examination of a set of charity accounts unless they have followed all these requirements.

An independent examiner's report provides a 'negative assurance'. If the examination is satisfactory, the independent examiner's report declares that:

- no evidence was found of lack of accounting records;
- neither of the accounts failing to comply with the records;
- nor of accounts failing to comply with the Act;
- nor are there other matters that need to be disclosed.

However, such a declaration can only be made after following 10 stages of Charity Commission Directions, so it is not simply a case of the examiner saying casually that no problems were spotted. The examiner's report has to cover a number of issues prescribed by the Regulations, so it will usually need a whole page. For most smaller charities an independent examination provides very effective scrutiny which goes much further than the 'informal audits' of the past, but which can be carried out without needing a registered auditor.

Selecting an independent examiner

Independent examiners come from a wide range of backgrounds, including accountants, bankers, engineers, staff of community accountancy projects and experienced charity treasurers acting as independent examiners to other charities. Some work professionally and thus charge a fee, but this is usually a good deal less than the cost of a full audit; however, many independent examiners, especially those acting for the smallest charities, work on a voluntary basis or charge only a nominal fee.

There are two kinds of independent examiner – an ordinary examiner (described in table 8.1 as an 'independent examiner of the charity's choice') and a professionally-qualified independent examiner.

Ordinary independent examiners

In England and Wales ordinary independent examiners can act for charities of up to £250,000 income. In Scotland, they can only be used where the accounts are on a receipts and payments basis (so the income must be under £100,000, although this will increase to £250,000 for accounting years starting from April 2011). In Northern Ireland, the Act allows ordinary independent examiners to act for any charity up to £100,000 income.

An 'ordinary' independent examiner is defined in law as 'an independent person who is reasonably believed by the charity trustees to have the requisite ability and practical experience to carry out a competent examination of the accounts' (this definition applies throughout the UK).

In such cases, no specific qualification is required, but clearly the person must have a good understanding of accounts, and charity accounts in particular. However, there can be certain concerns about the issues of 'requisite ability' and 'practical experience'. Even amongst accountants, only a few firms specialise in charities, and others can easily be caught out by all the requirements. Where people are acting informally as independent examiners there is wide ignorance of the new regime, for example some 'informal auditors' are doing just as they did in the past but simply putting 'independent examiner' after their name – this is illegal.

The issue of independence is also very important: in the past some 'informal audits' have been carried out by funders, landlords or close relatives of trustees, where there is clearly insufficient independence. It should be noted that an independent examiner must always be an individual: there is no provision for independent examination reports to be signed by a firm.

Whilst there is no legal requirement to have any specific qualification in order to be an independent examiner to smaller charities, Charity Commission guidance stresses the need for trustees to check that a prospective independent examiner really does have the appropriate competence, and a relevant qualification is certainly recommended for charities of more than £100,000 income.

Professionally-qualified independent examiners

For charities above £250,000 income in England and Wales, or £100,000 in Northern Ireland, or in Scotland a charity of any size where the accounts are on an accruals basis, the accounts must be examined by a professionally-qualified independent examiner. This is defined as 'an independent person' who holds one of a number of qualifications listed in the Charities Act 1993 (as amended). The person must be a qualified member of one of the following bodies:

- Institute of Chartered Accountants in England and Wales (ICAEW)
- Institute of Chartered Accountants of Scotland (ICAS)
- Institute of Chartered Accountants in Ireland (ICAI)
- Association of Chartered Certified Accountants (ACCA)
- Association of Authorised Public Accountants (AAPA)
- Association of Accounting Technicians (AAT)
- Association of International Accountants (AIA)
- Chartered Institute of Management Accountants (CIMA)
- Institute of Chartered Secretaries and Administrators (ICSA)
- Chartered Institute of Public Finance or Accountancy (CIPFA)
- Association of Charity Independent Examiners (ACIE).

This list includes the six chartered accountancy bodies, several other accountancy bodies, broader professional bodies such as ICSA, and the ACIE, which was established specifically to provide advice, training and qualifications for independent examiners. For a charity looking to find an experienced independent examiner, ACIE can provide lists of full members (for contact details see *Useful addresses*).

In the case of the ACIE, the Act specifies that the person must be a Fellow (holding the ACIE's highest qualification – FCIE) in order to act for a charity of more than £250,000 in England and Wales. However, most of the bodies on the list have specific rules which members must meet before they can act as an independent examiner (for example, they may insist that members hold a practising certificate, and this may apply even to act as an ordinary independent examiner).

It is possible to be a professionally-qualified independent examiner but still be a volunteer – but of course independently examining the accounts of a charity of more than £250,000 is a demanding process which will take a good deal of time, and only a few people holding the necessary qualifications would be able to do this voluntarily. In general, a charity must expect to pay a fee to an independent examiner, but in most cases this will be less than an audit fee.

Full audit

For a charity with an income of more than £500,000 (or a lower limit if the charity has substantial assets on its balance sheet – see table 8.2), the accounts must be subject to a full audit by a firm of registered auditors. (This is more than just being a qualified accountant – registered auditors must meet specified criteria and are subject to extensive professional monitoring.)

An audit report goes further than an independent examination; an audit report, if satisfactory, states that in the auditor's opinion the accounts give a 'true and fair view' of the charity's position. (This is for accruals accounts. In the rare event of a full audit of accounts on a receipts and payments basis, the auditor declares that they are 'properly presented'.)

The precise terms of the audit are slightly different according to whether the charity is a company, but in all cases a charity audit goes a good deal further than a general audit. For example, the regulations under the Charities Act require the auditor to state whether the accounts have been prepared in accordance with the methods and principles in the Charities SORP.

Selecting an auditor

To find an auditor you will always need to use a firm of accountants who are also registered auditors (although some accountants in practice on their own are recognised as audit firms). The key thing is to find a firm appropriate to your size of organisation with reasonable experience with charities and voluntary organisations.

You can start from local directories (such as Yellow Pages), ask for recommendations from other local charities, or approach the relevant professional accountancy bodies (see *Useful addresses*), most of which offer a referral service for organisations seeking an accountant. They may also be able to give you details of charity specialists in your area.

All UK registered auditors will be regulated by one of the first four bodies in the list above (ICAEW, ICAS, ICAI, ACCA). Internet searches may also help, and it is worth looking for advertisements in specialist charity sector magazines. Also, a body such as ACIE has a number of members who are charity auditors but joined ACIE because they specialise in smaller charities and also act as independent examiners.

Either way, you must normally expect to pay proper fees for accountants' time and costs. Some firms have lower rates for charities, but an audit always involves considerable expenses, and with charity accounts now forming a specialist field, free charity audits are nowadays extremely rare. Because of the issues of different funds, and all the notes needed to comply with the SORP, and the different sorts of income in the sector, an audit of a charity is typically much more work than a business audit of the same size. In fact, non-charitable companies are not nowadays generally required to have an audit unless their income is at least £6.5 million, so those firms of accountants who continue to provide audit services below this level will often be paying significant fees to maintain their audit registration specifically because of their charity audit work.

Some charities seeking a full audit ask two or three firms to tender, but you must be clear about what you are seeking, what information you will supply, and the timescales involved (remember many groups have a 31 March year end, so charity accountants tend to be very busy in the late spring, summer and early autumn). But do not just choose the cheapest figure – look at whether the firm really has the expertise to understand your charity.

Issuing the accounts to others

Whenever you are asked to send a copy of your accounts (for example with a funding application), you must always provide:

- the annual report (signed by the trustees);
- the annual accounts (signed by the trustees);
- the independent report on the accounts (signed by the auditor or independent examiner).

Once everything is complete and signed, it is worth getting enough copies made for your trustees, members, funders and others who may need to see the accounts – normally they are photocopied as a single document. A photocopied or printed signature is fine, so long as the name and date of approval are clear. (With increasing concerns about identity fraud, some trustees and independent examiners prefer just to sign the original set of accounts held by the charity, but with a printed signature on all circulated copies; such accounts are accepted by the Charity Commission).

Remember that, as a charity, your annual report and accounts form a public document, and anyone is entitled to see them (if necessary you can make a small charge to cover photocopying and postage) and for most registered charities in England and Wales, a scanned version of your report and accounts will be available to anyone on the Charity Commission's website.

However, the accounts should never be copied to anyone external until you have all three elements – the annual report, the accounts and the independent report – complete and signed (many funders will, quite rightly, reject unsigned accounts or accounts without the independent report, because legally they are no more than draft documents). If your accounts are not complete and you need to send accounts urgently to someone such as a prospective funder or donor, it is much better to send the previous year's accounts – perhaps with a covering letter explaining recent developments – rather than to send incomplete accounts for the current year.

9 Management accounts and budgets

As shown in chapter 2, accounts are not just a legal requirement at year end, they are vital for making day to day financial decisions in a charity. So, although the structure of your books needs to relate to the legal requirements, this is hardly their main purpose. In a well-run organisation, the largest use of information from the books is for ongoing financial monitoring and for decisions by trustees throughout the year.

Presenting information internally

Taking information from the books and presenting it in a form for internal decisions is the field of *management accounting*. Management accounting in a charity is also concerned with monitoring figures against budgets, analysing the cost-effectiveness of different approaches and handling issues of cashflow.

In a small charity, few people use the term 'management accounts' – most treasurers just talk about giving a current financial report – but the way you provide such information to the trustees has a huge effect on their ability to take meaningful decisions.

Traditionally, in many small charities you will hear something like the following exchange at trustees' meetings.

Chair: And now we come to the treasurer's report. Joe – can you give us an update on how we are doing?

Treasurer: Many thanks. I'm pleased to say we've got £273.29 in the current account and £1,503.50 in the deposit account, so we're doing quite well – we had over £200 in from the sponsored walk. But we've got some bills coming in next month so we mustn't get complacent – although I hear Sue has managed to get a new grant from a local trust, so that will help.

Sue: Yes, but we need to bear in mind that the new grant is specifically for play equipment.

Chair: Well that's very helpful, I'm sure the treasurer will make a note of that, and thank you once again, Joe, for all you do to keep our finances in such good order.

As a form of management accounting, this is almost useless. Apart from other factors, very few people can take in financial information that is only given verbally. But, more seriously, knowing how much is in the bank is only important if there are tight cashflow issues – a summary of income and expenditure, plus balances on each fund, will often communicate much more, especially if the income and expenditure is shown with actual figures compared with budgets.

Furthermore, as indicated by Sue's comment, this treasurer seems very vague about restricted funds (see chapter 3). As we have seen, fund accounting is not just an issue to sort out at year end to meet the charity accounting rules. It must be possible for the trustees to know at any time the resources available in each fund separately if they are to make proper decisions.

Using budgets

Budgets versus expenditure limits

Budgets are a vital tool in management accounting, but people use the word 'budget' in different ways:

- as an estimated income and expenditure account for next year (as in 'the budget of the charity was approved last night') – this is the way 'budget' is most often used in management accounts;
- as a target for the level of income or expenditure against a given account heading – one line within a budget statement in the first sense (as in 'our budget income from services is £3,000');
- as an agreed level of expenditure that can be incurred by the budget holder without further approval (as in 'I have been given a budget of up to £400 to spend on stationery').

So it is important to be clear with others what you mean. If the trustees approve a budget statement in the first sense it is simply a target – it does not necessarily mean they are giving authority for all the expenditure shown in the budget without further discussion. Also, some people used to public sector budget controls think they have to spend to the limit of a budget before year end. This may occasionally be true with a time-limited restricted fund but normally, in a charity, avoiding unnecessary expenditure means that more resources are left for future work.

Of course, as we saw in chapter 6, the trustees need to give delegated authority for the treasurer or finance officer to pay certain normal bills without individual discussion. Also, for certain costs you may want to give a senior member of staff the authority to spend up to a certain amount per year. But it is best to use a term such as 'authorised expenditure' to cover such policies. For example, the trustees may have agreed a budget statement that gives £750 as the estimated training expenditure in the coming year. However, the policy on incurring training expenses might be quite different, with delegated authority for small amounts, but still needing trustees' approval to spend over £200 on any single training event.

Preparing budget statements

As we noted, a finance report at a trustees' meeting is of little use if it only gives the bank balances, but even a report of actual income and expenditure does not tell people much unless they have some basis of comparison. You could simply make comparisons with last year, but in a fast-changing organisation this is not always relevant. Comparing actual figures against budgets is usually the best tool.

So, in a well-run charity, towards the end of the financial year the treasurer or finance officer will prepare a draft budget for discussion by trustees, showing for each line of income how much the charity reasonably expects to receive next year, and for each line of expenditure, an estimate of the costs. A draft budget looks just like an income and expenditure account (or receipts and payments account), but the figures are estimates for the future, rather than actual figures from the past. Where there are several funds (see *Funds in management accounts*, page 123) a separate budget statement is needed for each fund.

Some lines on the budget will be easy to determine, for example income from a known grant or expenditure on a fixed rent. Other items can be calculated quite accurately, for example salaries linked to specific scales (but with salaries, remember to allow both for inflationary rises *and* for individual staff moving to higher points on a scale, and do not forget the employer's national insurance (NI) on top). However, some income lines, such as 'fundraising', can be very hard to predict accurately in a small charity – these uncertainties need to be highlighted.

If you have inter-fund transfers, such as for management fees or contributions to overheads (see chapter 3), remember to include a line in the budget for these. The management fee is a certainly an expense of the fund or project, and it will leave other funds in deficit if the transfer is not made. Alternatively, if all overheads are charged directly to each fund, remember to include the share of overheads in the project budget.

On the other hand, a project sometimes has a specific subsidy from another fund, allowing you to show a funds transfer on the income side of the budget.

Many people think that budget statements have to balance, but there are three possibilities:

- surplus budget: planned income > planned expenditure
- deficit budget: planned income < planned expenditure
- balanced budget: planned income = planned expenditure

A surplus budget is essential if you need to build up reserves (see chapter 4). On the other hand, if a project has funds brought forward from the previous year, which are now to be spent, a deficit budget for the coming year is quite normal.

When preparing a draft budget, it is often best to put the estimates together and present the draft to the trustees for discussion, even if there is a large surplus or deficit. If the draft shows an unacceptable deficit, the trustees can then discuss what expenditure to cut, or they can resolve to increase income (thus creating a case for fundraising). If you present a draft budget that balances, they may simply approve it without serious discussion.

Since a budget statement is based on estimates, you need to be clear about any assumptions used. All budget statements can be optimistic or cautious (pessimistic); an optimistic budget assumes good levels of income and modest costs; a cautious budget allows for the highest levels of expenditure that might be needed but only assumes modest income. But if you prepare a pessimistic budget to make the case for more funds, make sure everyone realises the expenditure figures are worst cases and that they do not represent approved levels of expenditure.

Like the accounts themselves, budgets can be prepared on an accruals or a receipts and payments basis (see chapter 2). This makes a big difference when budgeting for capital items. In an accruals-based budget the cost of capital items will be spread over several years with a provision for depreciation each year, but on the receipts and payments basis, the full cost of a capital item is shown in the budget for the year when the purchase is made, with no cost in later years. Alternatively, some charities take fixed asset costs entirely out of normal management accounts and have a separate budget for capital expenditure.

In particular, when drawing up budgets for fundraising bids, many funders dislike seeing 'depreciation' and prefer to see capital costs and operating costs listed separately.

Using budgets in management accounts

If a realistic budget statement has been agreed, the best way of presenting interim financial reports is by showing actual figures against budgets, as in figure 9.1. In many cases, computerised accounting systems allow you to enter budget figures, so they can automatically generate reports of actuals against budgets. However, do make sure your reports add on the balance brought forward from last year in order to show the current balance of the fund – this is vital in knowing what is actually available to spend.

Some people like to add a column for the *budget variance* – the difference between the actual figure and the budget figure – this can be given as an amount in pounds either over or under, although many people find it easier to interpret when the variance is given as a percentage. This is calculated as follows:

$$\text{Budget Variance (\%)} = \frac{\text{Actual} - \text{Budget}}{\text{Budget}} \times 100$$

(However, you must then have a non-zero budget amount on every line: if the budget is £0.00 then even if the expenditure is only £0.50, the overspend expressed as a percentage is infinity and any system will give you an error!)

You need to be clear about positive and negative variances: on the income side a positive variance is good; but on the expenditure side you hope for a negative variance (actual expenditure less than budget expenditure).

Adding variances means more columns on reports, so do be sure your trustees will understand this – knowing that 'The budget variance on stationery is −77.5%' may actually exclude people rather than help them.

More elaborate reports can most easily be produced using spreadsheets – in particular, your books will be kept to the penny, but budgets and other figures for decision making are normally easier to follow if rounded to the nearest £1. You may want to consider presenting information graphically where it will help trustees to understand the position more easily.

Figure 9.1 Example of a year end budget report to trustees

MIDSHAM COMMUNITY ASSOCIATION – GENERAL FUND BUDGET REPORT
Internal Report for Trustees Only **For trustees meeting April 2012**

Last Year: Actuals 2010/11 £		Current Year Budget 2011/12 £	Current Year Actual 2011/12 £
	Receipts		
467	Members' Subscriptions	500	534
10000	Council Grant	25000	25000
500	Miscellaneous Donations	400	429
0	Tax Reclaimed on Gift Aid	170	140
1103	Christmas Bazaar	1100	1732
71	Bank Interest	60	53
12141	TOTAL RECEIPTS	27230	27888
	Payments		
980	Administrator Salary	1200	1079
934	Heat and Light	1000	869
389	Rates, Water Rates, Cleaning	400	403
6981	Repairs and Maintenance	4000	3708
321	Stationery	300	291
783	Publicity Literature	1000	1781
1089	Postage and Telephone	1100	1237
0	Purchase of Minibus	18000	18000
200	Independent Examiner's Fee	200	200
171	Committee Travel Expenses	200	126
0	Contribution to Outreach Project	0	100
0	Contingency	50	0
11848	TOTAL PAYMENTS	27450	27794
293	SURPLUS (BUDGET: DEFICIT)	−220	94
80	Add: Balance brought forward at 1 April		373
373	Balance carried forward 31 March		467

Notes to trustees:

1. You have seen my reports on these lines at previous meetings showing progress over the year – this is now the year end budget report covering the full 12 months.

2. The left-hand column shows the figures used in our published receipts and payments account for 2010/11. The far right column shows the actual figures for the year to March 2012 (subject to any adjustments by our independent examiner). The Budget column shows the 2011/12 budget figures that we agreed in February 2011.

3. You will recall that we budgeted for a £220 deficit for the year, after allowing for the minibus purchase (supported by the one-off increase in the council grant). We felt we could meet a small deficit because we expected to carry forward about £300 (actually £373 in the end) from 2010/11.

4. However, we have actually made a small surplus of £94. The main gains are due to better than expected receipts from the Christmas Bazaar, and lower than expected costs for Administrator Salary (less overtime than expected) and for Heat and Light and Repairs. But you will see that several expenditures areas were higher than predicted, particularly Publicity Literature. The final cost of the minibus was exactly as per the quotation that we used for the budget. Because of the deal we got, so far we have not yet incurred any running costs for the minibus, but we will need to include these next year.

5. Note that these figures *only* cover the General Fund. I have not presented a report for the Outreach Fund as the project is still at an early stage and we haven't yet set budgets, but you will see we have transferred £100 from the General Fund towards this, as agreed in the funding conditions.

Jane Corrigan - Treasurer 04.04.12

Breaking down the income and expenditure

A key issue with budget statements is how much detail to show. For a very simple fund you might need just one income line and one expenditure line. However, for the fund representing the main work of the charity, you may need 10 or more income lines and perhaps up to 30 expenditure lines.

Large organisations sometimes use multi-level budgets with different degrees of summary, but this is rarely needed in a local charity. So try to ensure that the full budget for any fund can show income, expenditure and balances on one page (and certainly no more than two) in a normal font size.

Remember that, in order to monitor actual figures against budgets, every line will have to be maintained as a separate category in your books (see chapter 5), so the more categories you create, the more complex the bookkeeping. For example, if you have nine funds and they each have 30 kinds of expenditure, your books will need 270 expenditure accounts (9 × 30). This is not difficult with a computer system, but great care is needed to ensure that expenditure is posted correctly. Moreover, if everything is budgeted, you will then have 270 separate expenditure budgets to monitor. So try to keep things simple.

Funds in management accounts

As we are starting to see, budget reports are fairly straightforward for a single fund or project. But if a charity has nine funds – say a general fund and eight restricted funds – then the trustees are managing nine different resources. It is almost like running nine organisations. You may need to take time with new trustees to ensure that they appreciate this.

You therefore, ideally, need separate management accounts for each fund. But although it is possible to produce an income and expenditure report for each fund showing actual figures against budgets, this would mean your management accounts would run to at least as many pages as the number of funds – and people simply will not read them. The opposite extreme to the scenario presented at the start of the chapter – but which can have the same result – is where the treasurer or finance manager overwhelms the trustees with so much financial information that they remain dependent on the treasurer for any understanding. There are cases of larger charities where trustees routinely get a 30-page set of management accounts for each meeting. Occasionally this may be helpful if the trustees want to discuss a certain project in detail and compare it with other projects, but in most cases it is useless.

Some trustees from a commercial background say 'I can't follow this – I want to see one overall budget' but it simply does not make sense to mix income and expenditure for different funds in a single budget report. Knowing that you are underspent on the salaries budget across the whole charity does not mean you can take on a general administrator if the underspend is mainly due to a specific unfilled post in a restricted fund.

Usually the best compromise is to provide:

- a summary report showing the financial position of the whole charity, broken down by funds (but without trying to show budgets);
- detailed income and expenditure budget reports for one or two funds where key decisions are needed (a capable treasurer will consider what is important for a given meeting).

As regards the summary for the whole charity, many organisations find that once trustees are used to the statement of financial activities (SOFA) (see chapter 7) it can be very useful, not just at year end but also as a management report during the year. It shows immediately the split of resources between unrestricted and restricted funds, including the balances brought forward, and the income lines make it easy to distinguish what has come in through grants and donations, through trading and fees, and through investment income.

However, the SOFA lumps all the restricted funds together in one column, which means you may not easily spot an individual restricted fund that is close to being overspent. So another helpful way of presenting a summary of the whole charity is simply to show a line for each fund, as in figure 9.2: in fact the Charities SORP 2005 now requires a note on these lines to be included in year end accounts. This type of report also makes it easy to spot when there are still funds in hand on a project that has finished, so that appropriate decisions can be taken.

Frequency of reports and accounting periods

It is best to link your management accounts into the cycle of trustees' meetings. For example, if your accounting year starts on 1 April and the trustees would like to see quarterly reports on finances, having trustees' meetings in mid-July, mid-October, etc. may work well.

Figure 9.2   Example of a report summarising movements on all funds

MIDSHAM COMMUNITY ASSOCIATION – FUND MOVEMENTS REPORT 2011/12

BALANCE 01 Apr 11 £	FUND	INCOME £	EXPENSES £	TRANSFERS £	BALANCE 31 Mar 12 £
	UNRESTRICTED FUNDS				
2313	General Fund	27918	14444	100–	15687
2313	Totals for Unrestricted Funds	27918	14444	100–	15687
	RESTRICTED FUNDS				
0	Outreach Project	4713	4554	100	259
0	Play Equipment Fund	5000	0	0	5000
39	Midsham Disability Project	143	73	0	109
39	Totals for Restricted Funds	9856	4627	100	5368
	CAPITAL FUNDS				
120000	Buildings Reserve	0	0	0	120000
120000	Totals for Capital Funds	0	0	0	120000
122352	TOTALS FOR ALL FUNDS	37774	19071	0	141055

Note: This report is based on accruals accounting. The fund balances thus include fixed assets and debtors/creditors where applicable.

The figures here do not tie up exactly with the accounts in chapter 7 because two further funds are included in this example.

If you have monthly trustees' meetings it is worth asking whether you really need full management accounts every month, or whether bi-monthly or quarterly would suffice. Although finance is important, it is not the only issue to discuss. For a small charity, the change in the financial picture during just one month may not be significant.

Once you have established the cycle of reporting, you need to decide whether to divide the year into separate accounting periods, or whether 'year-to-date' reports will be best. For example, at the October trustees' meeting when you present figures for the second quarter (July–September) would it be best to show just the last three months' income and expenditure, or would it be more meaningful to show the year so far (April–September)?

To do separate reports for each quarter, you will need to close off your books, or select 'close of period' on your computer system at the end of each quarter. Figures for a single period are most useful with trading income, where you may need to monitor profitability for each period separately, but for general monitoring year-to-date figures can be more meaningful.

When producing reports for part of the year, you also need to decide whether to show part-year budgets or full-year figures. For example, at the nine-month point (April–December in this case) it can be useful to see whether you are over or under budget based on $^9/_{12}$ of the full-year budget. Other people prefer to show the full-year budget so it is clear (particularly on income) whether you are close to the full-year target. Another possibility is to show just the last period (October–December) against $^3/_{12}$ of the budget.

Computerised accounting systems will often give you a huge choice of reports of this kind: it is worth experimenting with the options and then settling on one format that suits your trustees.

Also, bear in mind that some funders will need you to report on a 12-month cycle that is different from your normal accounting year: this may mean combining period figures from two different accounting years.

Although management accounting reports based on comparisons of actual figures and budgets can be useful, they are often criticised for focusing too much on the past when, arguably, trustees should be focusing more on the future. But in preparing future budgets you will often need to be presenting three years' figures. For example, if it is January 2011 and you are preparing a budget for the year beginning 1 April 2011, you will not yet have the final figures for the current year (2010/11). So you may need to present:

- actual totals for last year (2009/10);
- budgets agreed for the current year (2010/11) – agreed a year ago;
- actual figures for the first nine months of the current year (April–December 2010);
- suggested budget for next year (2011/12).

However, this can mean a lot of numbers, and it is rarely possible for a full trustees' meeting to grapple with such detailed figures – such discussions may be better considered by a small group. There is also a tendency to set future budgets by applying a small percentage change to past budgets, which does not encourage the trustees to think in visionary terms. Some people advocate 'zero-based budgeting', where every budget starts from zero each year, and you ask 'what can we really expect to achieve next year?', starting from first principles.

Cashflow

Thinking about cashflow is a great way to focus on the future. We saw in chapter 4 the importance of cashflow planning for some charities. This is quite separate from normal budgeting, but where cashflow is tight your management accounts may need to include cashflow projections.

A cashflow forecast is usually presented as a table, showing the expected money in and money out each month on a cumulative basis (this must be done on a receipts and payments basis, even if the charity is otherwise doing accruals accounts, because it is the cash in and out that matters). Alternatively, it can help to present the cashflow as a graph.

A spreadsheet can be helpful in putting together the figures, but you cannot expect to generate this automatically from an accounting system, since your books (whether manual or computerised) will only tell you about the past. Figures from the past may help your projections, but only someone with a good knowledge of the expected future income and expenditure streams and the timings can prepare the forecast.

When doing a cashflow forecast for a new project, the largest negative figure determines how much money you must have in hand from somewhere else to support the cashflow. For example, if the forecast goes to −£10,000 at its lowest point, the charity must not undertake the work unless it can support the project with £10,000 of working cash from elsewhere (preferably more, to allow for contingencies). Also, the trustees must be satisfied that the risks of the project do not jeopardise other funds.

The working cash could come from other funds of the charity, or via a loan (but if the charity considers borrowing, do look carefully at your governing document to make sure the trustees have the power to borrow). Alternatively, when you demonstrate the cashflow problems, you may be able to persuade the funder to pay earlier, particularly if it is keen for you to do the work. The latest HM Treasury guidance to funders of third sector organisations indicates that payment in advance can often be justified as good value for money.

If cashflow is the main issue, your management accounts will want to focus on actual cash received and paid out each month compared with the projected cashflow from the project plan. Frequent trustees' meetings may be vital to monitor this closely, and if problems occur, expenditure may have to be postponed. If there is any chance that the charity may run out of funds completely, take professional advice urgently, or the trustees could find they are acting illegally.

Cashflow planning is usually done in relation to a whole charity, rather than fund by fund, as you will normally have one set of bank accounts for the whole organisation. Charities often rely on higher balances in one area to support projects that are temporarily in deficit, and this is an effective means of cashflow management. However, care must be taken on this: if the project in deficit does not recover, the trustees could find that they have spent restricted funds on a completely unrelated purpose, and so they could be in breach of trust. Also, if such arrangements mean that a restricted fund loses out on interest, there is a case for regarding the arrangement formally as an 'internal loan', where the fund with the cashflow difficulties might make a transfer to reimburse another fund for interest lost.

Supporting a charity through a major cashflow crisis is perhaps one of the ultimate tests for a treasurer or finance officer.

Communicating accounts meaningfully

Producing management accounts has no value unless they are meaningful to the readers. You cannot expect trustees to make informed decisions unless they understand the information they are given.

Pure verbal reports are not much use, but neither is a large pile of papers with numerous figures and few comments. Try to get management accounts circulated before the meeting if possible. At the meeting, talk people through what you have provided (but without commenting on every figure) and encourage questions. With larger meetings, projecting the figures can help (but not if you go through slides too quickly for people to follow them). It can be useful to have one trustees' meeting each year – perhaps the annual budget-setting meeting – when someone explains the overall structure of the charity's accounts and the purpose of each fund.

Try to use meaningful names for accounts and funds and carefully consider font sizes, paper colours and other readability issues (and use a consistent format from one meeting to the next). Graphical presentations can help, particularly if trustees are being asked to decide between two options – if you are an experienced spreadsheet user this will not be difficult. If any trustees have disabilities affecting what they can read, you need to take this into account – ask them directly how they would like the information presented.

However, do bear in mind that spending hours each month or quarter reformatting your accounts in spreadsheets can add enormously to the work of the treasurer or finance officer, so be wary of taking on ever-increasing demands that you cannot sustain. If the standard printouts from your computer-based accounting system can serve as management accounts, it is obviously much easier.

10 Accruals accounting

As explained in chapter 2, once a charity's total income (across all funds) exceeds the relevant threshold, the final accounts must be prepared on an accruals basis and presented in SORP format. If the charity is a company, the final accounts must be on an accruals basis whatever the income. For charities which are *not* companies (this includes CIOs) accruals accounts are only compulsory once the income reaches £250,000 (England and Wales) or £100,000 in Scotland or Northern Ireland (though the Scottish limit will go up to £250,000 for years starting from April 2011.) (In fact, many charities will want to do this at lower levels of income to give a more professional look to the accounts.)

For many treasurers and finance staff, the Statement of Recommended Practice (SORP) format is not the problem: once you understand the idea of fund accounting, the layout of the statement of financial activities (SOFA) and balance sheet is quite logical. What often needs more thought, if you do not have a formal accounting background, is making the correct postings in the books (or on your computerised accounting system), for items such as debtors, creditors and fixed assets.

Who does what?

If you feel the accruals principles are too much for you, it is possible to keep the books during the year on a receipts and payments basis, and then pay an accountant at year end to convert everything to accruals for the final accounts. Accountants are used to working on this basis, and it is probably better to use this option than to try accruals accounting if you do not understand the principles at all.

However, if you do this, it means that your internal management accounts may end up looking very different from your final accounts. For example, you may think a fund had money in hand at year end, but once the accountant has adjusted for a creditor, the fund may be in deficit in the final accounts. On the other hand, a fund might appear fully spent when calculated on a receipts and payments basis, but once a fixed asset purchase is capitalised (see *Fixed assets,* page 138), the fund may look as though very little has been spent.

So, even if you do not feel able to keep your day-to-day books on the accruals basis, it is vital for charity treasurers and finance workers to have at least some understanding of the accruals principles used by your accountant to make these adjustments. Otherwise you may have to ask your trustees to approve accounts you do not understand yourself. Moreover, if you send out accounts that you do not understand, how will you deal with queries from funders?

It follows that if you can get on top of the basic principles of accruals accounting, there is a lot to be said for keeping your books on this basis. All but the smallest computer-based accounting systems are designed to use the principles of accruals accounting. For example, you should be able to post an invoice from a supplier and your subsequent payment of the invoice as two separate events with separate dates. (Between these dates – when the invoice is entered but the payment is not yet made – the invoice is included as a creditor in the balance sheet, but the expenditure has been charged to the fund concerned. We say the expenditure has been 'recognised' even though money has not yet gone out of the charity's bank account.) So it is not necessarily difficult.

On the income side, the same concept allows an accounting system to maintain a 'sales ledger' – which is very useful if your charity provides any kind of service under contract and you have to keep track of unpaid invoices you have issued. Also, it is worth noting that if your charity has to register for VAT (see chapter 11), the books *must* be kept on an accruals basis, unless the charity has agreement to operate the VAT cash accounting system.

Standard bookkeeping texts offer much more on the principles of accruals accounting concepts than we can cover in a short book (see *Further reading*) – in fact, accounting textbooks do not normally even mention receipts and payments accounts. However, the rest of this chapter summarises the key issues and gives some examples, and then explains how accruals accounts link with accounting standards.

Concepts of accruals accounts

The key principle of accruals accounts is that they show the *income due* to the charity (or to a certain fund) during the year and the costs and *expenses incurred*. This is clearly a better way of understanding the charity's resources and demands than simply recording cash in and out. For more on this and some of the differences, see *Accruals or receipts and payments?*, on page 27.

Showing income and expenditure in terms of revenue earned and costs incurred has several important implications.

- *Accruals accounts may need estimates and judgements.* For example, choosing a depreciation policy or deciding whether to include a promised donation as a debtor. These will affect postings in the records and hence the final figures on the SOFA and balance sheet. There are no right and wrong answers: it is a matter of judgement, and depending on the judgements made, different sets of accounts could be produced for the same charity.

  However, if you were to make ludicrous judgements, your auditor or independent examiner would have to give a qualified report. In many cases the SORP gives guidance on such issues: many paragraphs are concerned with the criteria for 'recognising income' (deciding what income should be included), and for 'recognising expenses'.

- *Accruals accounts must give a 'true and fair' view.* This is always the aim when judgements and policies are made. Accounting standards are very important in this respect in setting the principles to be used in such judgements – these include not just the SORP but also more general accounting standards (see below). Such judgements ultimately have to be agreed by the trustees, on the basis of trying to ensure that the accounts give a true and fair view of the charity's affairs, but in most cases the trustees will be guided by the recommendations of their treasurer, finance officer or accountant.

  Accountants spend a lot of time studying the phrase 'true and fair', but for the layperson it is best to take the words at face value. For example, if your charity had received a bill for £10,000 just before year end for costs it had incurred during the year, it would hardly be 'fair' to show accounts with £2,500 in hand if, in reality, you would be £7,500 in deficit once this bill was paid. Receipts and payments accounts may show a 'true record' of money received and paid out, but they will rarely be 'fair' in the sense of this example.

- *The four fundamental accounting concepts are assumed to apply to the accounts* (unless there is a specific note to the contrary).

  1. The *going concern basis* – unless stated otherwise, accounts are prepared on the basis that the organisation has sufficient resources to continue. This is crucial for issues such as depreciation of fixed assets (see page 138) – by spreading the cost of a major purchase over several years, you are assuming the organisation will continue to exist for that time.

  2. The *accruals basis* – income and costs appear in the accounts as they are accrued (as they are earned and incurred).

3. *Consistency* – where judgements are made, they should be consistent each year.

4. *Prudence* – when in doubt, accounts should never be over-optimistic (though prudence cannot override the first three criteria).

* *The concept of 'materiality'.* This applies to all figures in the SOFA, balance sheet and notes. It means that you do not have to worry about where to show something if it is too small to be material to readers of the accounts. But care is needed when applying this to charities. For example, an item that is small in relation to the charity as a whole may be material in relation to a certain fund. Even a very small payment to a trustee will almost always be material because it could affect the issue of trustees' independence and the test of public benefit (see chapter 1).

The impact of accounting standards

In order to give a true and fair view, accruals accounts should take account of *all relevant published accounting standards* in terms of the principles and judgements used. Although the Charities SORP will be the most prominent standard, other more general standards are also relevant. The most important standards used in the UK are called FRSs (financial reporting standards) and each FRS deals with a specific accounting issue which could potentially apply in *any* sector. For example, FRS17 deals with how organisations should account for commitments regarding employees' pensions – where there could be liabilities many years ahead.

However, many large companies are now required to use international accounting standards (IASs) or international financial reporting standards (IFRSs) and under a process of 'convergence' UK standards are gradually being brought into line – it is likely that the next major revision of the SORP will link charity accounting into the IFRS framework. (Note: Do not confuse IASs with ISAs – international standards on auditing. If your charity is subject to a full audit – see chapter 8 – ISAs will already affect the work of your auditor, even if the charity's accounts are entirely based on UK standards. So occasionally an auditor may mention the need for extra work to comply with ISAs – but ISAs do not affect the presentation of your accounts.)

To save small organisations having to know about numerous separate FRSs and other standards, the main principles are currently brought together in a document known as the FRSSE (*Financial Reporting Standard for Smaller Entities* – usually pronounced 'frizzy' – see *Further reading*). For all but the very largest charities, the combination of FRSSE and SORP will almost always be sufficient (the FRSSE can normally be used by organisations of up to £6.5 million income).

Accruals transactions

Although people sometimes imply that accruals and receipts and payments accounting are totally distinct, the vast majority of day to day transactions, such as receiving a donation or paying wages, will be entered in the same way in both systems.

Similarly, certain transfers that have no net income or expenditure to the charity will be the same with receipts and payments or accruals. These include transactions for moving money between bank accounts, drawing petty cash and most inter-fund transfers.

Where differences arise, they mainly relate to debtors, creditors and fixed assets. Even with receipts and payments accounts, you need to keep track of these items, in order to include them on the statement of assets and liabilities (SOAL). But the big difference with accruals accounting is that the value of debtors, creditors and fixed assets is directly included in the value of relevant funds. This can give rise to transactions that do not involve movements of money but which affect the balances of funds.

To record these correctly, use of double entry bookkeeping is strongly recommended (see chapter 5), but if you are using a computer-based accounting system, you can probably make many entries without needing to understand debits and credits. However, to cover all cases, including manual books, we use the format of debits (DR) and credits (CR) in the following examples. If your system includes provision for entry of 'journals', *any* transaction at all can be entered on this basis – though most systems provide considerably easier ways of entering common transactions such as raising an invoice.

Money owed to the charity (debtors)

If there is an increase in the amount of money owed to a charity (the debtors figure), for example if you suddenly hear on 5 December 2011 that someone has died and the charity is entitled to receive a £12,000 legacy, you will need to make an entry in the books to record this income, even though it may be many months before the money is physically received. The transaction to post would be:

5 Dec 2011	DR	Debtors	£12,000
	CR	Donated income	£12,000

This appears as £12,000 income to the fund. The income appears on the SOFA, balanced by the debtors figure on the balance sheet. This is correct: the charity is legally entitled to this money, it is part of your resources and your trustees can decide how to spend it. (But if cashflow is tight, you might want to wait until the money comes in before spending it.)

When the legacy is finally paid over, perhaps not until well into the next accounting year, take care not to record it as new income: you have already 'recognised' the income. All that happens in the new year is that the debtor is converted to money in the bank:

| 13 Sep 2012 | CR | Debtors | £12,000 |
| | DR | Bank | £12,000 |

The effect of this is that the bank balance goes up by £12,000 and the debtors figure is reduced by £12,000. The balance of the debtors account is now zero (assuming there are no other debtors). Since the income was recorded previously, the fund balances are unaffected.

Money owed by the charity (creditors)

Creditors are typically unpaid bills at year end. For example, assume that on 23 March 2012 you received a bill for £775 for gas consumed, but this was not paid by your year end of 31 March. Clearly this was part of the expenses of running the charity in the last year and, for a true and fair view, it must be 'recognised' as an expense. You can post this by entering:

| 23 Mar 2012 | CR | Creditors | £775 |
| | DR | Heat/light expenses | £775 |

(If the gas bill is normally apportioned between funds, there may be several debits to different expenditure accounts.)

The balance of the relevant fund(s) has now gone down by £775 because of this expense. The expenditure appears on the SOFA, and is balanced by the creditors figure on the balance sheet.

In the following year when you pay the bill remember that, although you are writing a cheque, this is not new expenditure – the expenditure was included last year. You are simply transferring money out of the bank to settle a creditor. So post this as:

| 23 Apr 2012 | DR | Creditor | £775 |
| | CR | Bank | £775 |

The bank balance has gone down and, if this was the only creditor, the creditors balance (which was negative – in credit) is now back to zero. But the fund balances are unchanged in the new year – the expense was 'recognised' last year.

Sometimes you will need to provide for a creditor even though you have not received a bill by year end because you know that the charity has incurred the relevant costs – such entries are often called 'accruals'. The most common example is the fee due to your auditor or independent examiner – even though it may not be billed until many months after year end, the expense relates to the year of the accounts concerned. If you are posting all entries yourself and preparing the final SOFA and balance sheet, remember to get confirmation of this figure before you close your books (and remember to include VAT if applicable).

Prepayments and deferred income

The converse can apply where money is paid out in the year *before* the one to which the expenditure applies. For example, you might have to pay a large deposit to hire a venue for an event next year. This is called a *prepayment* and appears as a debtor on the balance sheet.

Conversely, you will sometimes receive income in advance, for example a grant paid early but with a clear condition that it cannot be spent until next year. Although you will have the money in the bank, the charity is not yet legally entitled to it, so it is balanced by a creditor on the balance sheet. The logic is that if the charity closed down at the end of the current year, the money would have to be repaid. You are not entitled to the income until next year. Creditors related to amounts received in advance are often called *deferred income*.

Estimated prepayments and accruals

To make matters harder, prepayments and accruals sometimes have to be estimated. For example, if it has been two months since your last gas bill, then at year end you owe a certain amount for gas even though you have not yet been billed: this requires an estimated accrual if the accounts are to allow for the full year's energy bills. Or you may have paid an insurance premium at the end of January for the following 12 months: strictly speaking if you have a 31 March year end, only two months of this payment relates to the current year and 10 months is a prepayment towards insurance for the year ahead. For really precise accounting, you need to estimate these figures and post appropriate accruals and prepayments.

At one time accountants placed much effort in calculating and entering such adjustments. But often a lot of work can be saved by applying the principle of materiality – would it affect a reader of the accounts? If you were running a steel works, the accrued energy costs at year end could make a big difference to a company's final accounts, but for the vast majority of small to medium-sized charities the effect of such adjustments will be too small to be material. So long as you have paid four quarterly gas bills in the year, small adjustments at the start and end of the year will have little impact on the total picture.

Posting prepayments and accruals can become complex, and if you have to enter these you may need help, particularly if estimated amounts then need to be adjusted the following year. But remember they are only needed when the effect is material. Whatever you do, try to follow the principle of consistency from year to year – however, if you realise that the practice in past years was giving a seriously misleading result and thus decide to make a change of accounting policy, remember this needs a note of explanation in the final accounts (see line (c) in table 7.5).

Fixed assets

Fixed assets need some thought, but the key thing to bear in mind is that if you are buying furniture, equipment or anything with a life of several years, the cost needs to be spread over several accounting years – this is known as *depreciation*. The depreciation figure in the accounts is a measure of how much fixed assets were 'used up' in the year concerned.

For example, if you spend £1,500 on computer equipment and you expect it to last about three years, you will probably want to show £500 of expenditure in the accounts for three successive years. On the balance sheet, the equipment appears under 'Fixed assets' with a value of £1,500 when first bought, and the value goes down as the depreciation is charged: so the value will be £1,000 after the first year, £500 after the second year and £0 after the third year. (This is 'straight-line depreciation' – there are other methods.)

The SORP does not require any specific depreciation policy: it is up to the trustees to make reasonable judgements based on the expected life of assets bought, but try to avoid anything too complex or having too many different rates. However, it is normal to have a *capitalisation limit*, where purchases for less than a certain amount (typically £250 for a small charity) are entered in full when the purchase is made. To depreciate items costing less than the limit, even if they might last several years, will rarely be material.

For everything above the capitalisation limit, you need a *fixed asset register*, where you record the item at the time of purchase (this is also useful for insurance purposes, though if you are using it for this purpose, do not forget to list the smaller items, too). Then note each year's depreciation when you enter it in the books. Without this, it is almost impossible to enter depreciation correctly for something bought several years ago.

Consider a charity that buys a minibus for £18,000. The key thing to remember when you make the purchase is that, although you have written a cheque for this amount, you are simply converting money in the bank into assets of a different sort. So the entry in the books might be:

18 Jan 2012	CR	Bank	£18,000
	DR	Fixed assets – minibus	£18,000

The bank balance has gone down by £18,000 and the fixed assets have gone up by £18,000. As yet there has been no expenditure, and the fund balances are unaffected. If, for example, the minibus is funded by a special grant, the balance of the restricted fund will still show the full £18,000. The only change is that the assets of the fund now comprise a minibus instead of cash in the bank.

It is only when you enter depreciation that the fund goes down. If the minibus is to be depreciated at 25% for the first year, the depreciation at the end of that year will be:

31 Mar 2012	CR	Fixed assets – minibus	£4,500
	DR	Expenses – depreciation	£4,500

This does not affect the bank balance, but it does represent real expenditure on the SOFA. (This example assumes the common policy of charging a whole year's depreciation in the first year, regardless of how long the asset has been held.)

The depreciation expense account must be an expenditure category in the fund that is paying for the minibus. If this was a restricted fund specifically for the minibus purchase, the balance of the fund will reduce gradually over the years (rather than immediately after purchase). This is fully in accordance with the SORP, but sometimes needs explaining to those reading the accounts.

Applying the concepts – an exercise

In the light of the principles in this chapter, you may like to look back to the examples in figures 7.2 and 7.4, which show the accounts of the same charity on a receipts and payments basis and accruals basis. Taking into account the items on the SOAL at the start and end of the year, you might like to see if you can work from the receipts and payments accounts in figure 7.2 to get to the SOFA and balance sheet amounts in figure 7.4. Notice the differences in the fund balances.

11 Social enterprise, trading income and taxes

For many years charities have been encouraged to develop their sustainability by finding services that they can *sell*, rather than seeking to fund their work entirely through donated income, and the government is keen for third sector organisations (where appropriate) to provide services under contract to the public sector. In addition, many methods of fundraising ultimately come down to selling something to supporters (e.g. tickets for an event) rather than seeking pure donations.

In each of these situations, the charity is *trading*, as we saw in chapter 4. Such trading activities are often described as 'social enterprises' (see chapter 1, page 2 for more on this term). However, there are big differences in legal and tax terms between social enterprise activities operated by a charity (the subject of this chapter), and non-charitable social enterprises structured as Community Interest Companies (CICs), for example, which are taxed in the same way as normal businesses.

Even if such activities are only a small part of the organisation's total income, any charity treasurer or finance officer needs to understand the accounting implications of trading income – the biggest of which is tax.

Charities and tax

There are many ways in which tax works differently for charities as compared with individuals or businesses. Many of the complications relate to trading but there are also special tax rules in other areas (many of them beneficial), which can affect both income and expenditure.

There is a widespread myth that charities are not subject to tax. In fact the situation is much more varied, as shown in table 11.1.

Charity taxation is a complex field, and in a book of this size we can only highlight a few key issues that treasurers of smaller charities need to keep in mind. From table 11.1, it is clear that trading income is the area that most often gives rise to problems. For more guidance see *Further reading*, and bear in mind that the rules and thresholds change slightly each year. Some of the tax reliefs create special opportunities for fundraising – see chapter 12.

Table 11.1 Major taxes – issues for charities

Examples

A. No special reliefs for charities:
- Employer's national insurance (NI)
- Insurance premium tax

B. Some reliefs in specific situations:
- VAT (limited concessions for charities – growing slowly)
- Business rates (more extensive concessions)

C. General relief for most charitable work:
- Corporation tax   (on primary purpose trading)
- Income tax   (on investment income)
- Capital gains tax   (on investment gains)
- Inheritance tax   (on legacy income)

Understanding different funding channels

We have seen that a funder may potentially support a charity in two completely different ways:

- by *making a gift* to the charity (a grant or donation); or
- by *purchasing services* from the charity under a contract.

In the case of funds given to the charity it is usual to speak of a 'donation' if it is from an individual or a 'grant' if it is from an organisation, but the two terms mean the same thing. A grant may, of course, be subject to conditions on its use (sometimes running to many pages), in which case the grant income will certainly need to be allocated to a restricted fund. But ultimately, if a funder is providing resources to a charity without requiring anything in return (other than feedback and monitoring), the income needs to be treated for tax purposes as donated income.

As explained in chapter 4, the contract funding situation is very different – the funder is procuring services from the charity under what is essentially a commercial agreement. If the services are not up to the agreed standard, the funder could potentially sue the charity for breach of contract. But if the charity completes the work in accordance with the agreement, it is entitled to retain any surplus made. See figure 11.2 for more on these differences.

Figure 11.2   The two main funding channels

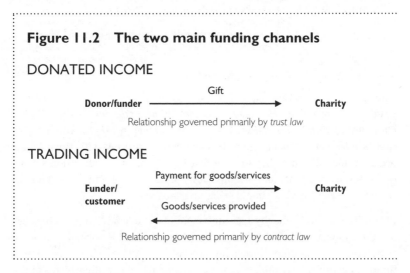

DONATED INCOME

Gift

Donor/funder ————————————➤ Charity

Relationship governed primarily by *trust law*

TRADING INCOME

Payment for goods/services

Funder/ ————————————➤ Charity
customer

Goods/services provided

◄————————————

Relationship governed primarily by *contract law*

Sadly there is much confusion on this issue; in fact, as explained in chapter 4, some funders are unclear themselves. Some service level agreements (SLAs) devote pages to the service provision, but when it comes to the section on money it may be so brief that it is not always clear whether a grant or a contract is intended.

This is very dangerous for both parties as it is not clear where the obligations lie, and moreover, there could be huge differences in the VAT position between a grant and a contract. Getting this wrong can seriously jeopardise the financial viability of a charity. Usually the grant/contract distinction will also affect whether the funds are restricted – see table 11.3.

Table 11.3   Accounting for grant and contract income

TREATMENT OF INCOME	UNRESTRICTED	RESTRICTED
DONATED INCOME	Only general donations can be unrestricted	**Grants for a specific purpose always restricted**
TRADING INCOME	**Normally unrestricted:** the only obligation is to provide the required goods/services: any surplus/deficit is retained by the charity	Only restricted if customers were promised that any surplus would be used for a specific purpose (e.g. A fundraising event for a specific project)

Ambiguity on funding channels is also contrary to HM Treasury's guidance *Improving Financial Relationships with the Third Sector: Guidance to Funders and Purchasers* (see *Further reading*), which states that public sector funders must be clear when working with third sector organisations whether they are seeking to develop an organisation's work (in which case a grant is normally best) or want to procure a service (in which case the funding should be contract-based).

Part of the task of a charity treasurer should include advising the trustees on the impact of any new funding, and this will normally involve reviewing any funding agreement before the trustees sign it. Where a funding agreement is ambiguous on this issue (or if any other terms of the agreement present serious problems) it is worth insisting that it must be amended before agreeing to sign – even if this means delaying a new project.

Types of trading income

In chapter 4 we explained that trading income means any income to the charity from selling goods or services (as opposed to donated income and investment income). We also saw that there are two distinct types of trading income:

- *primary purpose trading* – where the goods or services provided are directly part of the charity's objects;
- *trading for fundraising purposes* – where the goods or services provided are sold simply as a means of raising funds.

See chapter 4 for more on these terms and common examples. Most contract funding for the main work of a charity is likely to be primary purpose trading, but there are exceptions. For example, if a charity's objects are to provide relief for older people in a particular district, then a contract for an older persons' support project in that district would clearly be primary purpose trading. But if the charity then extended its services and accepted a contract to support older people from a *different* area, the second contract would be trading for fundraising purposes (even though it involved the same work) because the charity would be receiving fees for work outside its objects. (In such a case the charity might wish to seek approval for a change of objects to widen the area of benefit.)

However, primary purpose trading does not mean that the 'customer' has to be a public sector body. The purchasers may be the service users themselves: this is often the case with housing charities, charities providing fee-based training courses and welfare charities where clients may themselves pay for services under 'direct payments' schemes.

Whenever trading income is involved, there are two tax questions to consider.

- Should the charity be charging VAT on what it is selling?
- Is the charity liable to corporation tax if the activity makes a profit?

Charities and Value Added Tax

Most businesses, other than the very smallest, are VAT registered, which means that they have to charge VAT on what they sell, but they can reclaim the VAT on what they buy.

Purchases by the charity

Many people think that charities can also reclaim VAT but in most cases this is not possible because grants, donations and investment income do not count as trading income, and the ability to reclaim VAT only applies when an organisation is trading. So normally, whenever you buy anything, your charity will have to pay the supplier's price including VAT. In the books, few small charities therefore need to show VAT separately, and just enter all expenses at the total value including VAT.

Remember to bear VAT in mind when budgeting. (The examples in this chapter are based on VAT at 20% (from 2011) but always be sure to use the current figure). For example if you are quoted a price of £1,200 excluding VAT for a new photocopier, and you want to apply for a grant to cover the cost, you will need a grant of £1,440. The extra £240 is to cover the 20% VAT you pay to the supplier, but which the supplier passes on to the government. Across the sector, charities pay hundreds of millions of pounds of tax to the government in this way.

There are a few concessions for some items supplied to charities, but they only apply in certain fields – for example press advertisements and new buildings. When someone places an advertisement in a newspaper it would normally be subject to 20% VAT, but if the advertisement is placed by a charity, the newspaper company is allowed to charge you 0% VAT.

With buildings the rules are complex, and if you are considering major building work, it is important to get professional advice on the VAT position at an early stage. The general principle is that a new charity building (though not an extension or alteration) will be zero-rated for VAT (i.e. VAT will be charged at 0%) if it is used exclusively for 'non-business charitable purposes' – in other words, if the charitable work which takes place in the building is funded entirely by grants, donations or investment income. Once the level of business use exceeds 5% – for example, if more than 5% of the charity's work is funded by fees or contracts – this concession is likely to be lost, and the full 20% VAT will be charged on the construction price. (However, there are various ways of calculating the 5%, such as income, staff count or floor area.)

There is also a government grant scheme to refund the VAT on building repairs in the specific case of listed buildings registered as places of worship (the Listed Places of Worship Grant Scheme – see www.lpwscheme.org.uk) – but a range of conditions has to be met. However, it is important to note that this is a grant scheme: it does not affect the basic tax rules for VAT.

Goods and services sold by the charity

If your charity has any trading income, it is classed as a business for VAT purposes. In certain cases the charity will need to register for VAT, and charge VAT on what it sells. If this applies, you will need to separate out the VAT amounts in your books. Your trustees *must* apply to register for VAT if your total trading income (across all funds and projects) exceeds the VAT registration level (£70,000 in 2010/11, although the limit increases slightly each year). However, in calculating the total trading income, you can exclude sales which, if you were VAT registered, would be VAT-exempt (see below).

VAT registration is done through the relevant HM Revenue & Customs (HMRC) VAT registration office for your area (see www.hmrc.gov.uk for the addresses and guidance – registration is done by completing and returning form VAT1). Charities that do have to register for VAT are usually *VAT partially exempt* (because the grants and donations side is non-VATable), which makes the VAT issues more complex than in a normal business.

If this is the case, you will need further guidance – beyond the scope of this book – on VAT accounting. The aim of this section is simply to help you work out if your charity is safely below the VAT threshold. If you conclude that you do not need to register, you can ignore VAT issues in relation to income – but in that case remember to allow for all expenditure at prices including VAT. (If a charity has some trading income, but below the threshold, it is possible to register for VAT voluntarily, but there are few cases where you would gain by doing do. The main examples where voluntary registration is worth considering are where most or all of the sales would be zero-rated, e.g. if the charity derives substantial income from charity shops selling donated goods, or from sales of books and publications.)

Where an organisation is VAT registered, it must charge VAT at the appropriate rate on everything sold. In most cases this is bad news. For example, if you sell packs of Christmas cards at £4.00 each, and the charity becomes VAT registered, you would have to charge your supporters £4.80 (including 20% VAT – 80p – which you would pass on to the government). Alternatively, you could keep the price at £4.00 and absorb the VAT, but selling packs at £4.00 including 20% VAT works out as £3.33 plus 67p VAT, so you would lose 67p on each pack sold. A charity raising thousands of pounds through Christmas cards would be much worse off. (To convert a VAT-inclusive price to the VAT-exclusive amount, divide by 1.20 if VAT is at 20%. In this example £4.00 ÷ 1.20 = £3.3333 = £3.33 to the nearest 1p.)

On the other hand, if you were providing a service to your local authority, or to a normal VAT registered business, they would not mind if you had to add VAT, because they could reclaim it. So the implications of VAT depend enormously on your customer. Where a charity is doing work for a local authority it is often much better to do it under a contract where the work is subject to VAT, because then you can register for VAT and reclaim the VAT on the things you buy. If the work were grant funded, the charity would not be trading so you could not register for VAT, and therefore the VAT you spent on purchases would be irrecoverable. In such a case, doing work under a VATable contract rather than a grant can make funding go further (provided that you feel confident about accounting for a VAT registered charity).

'Irrecoverable VAT' – as illustrated in the previous paragraph – is a major problem for charities. On large projects it may be worth consulting a VAT specialist to see if there is any way round the issue – for example by persuading a funder to convert a grant to a contract, or by altering the balance of the charity's work to affect the calculation of 'non-business use' on a new building.

There are currently five categories of income for VAT purposes.

- Most goods and services are subject to *standard rate VAT* (currently 17·5% but increasing to 20% from 4th January 2011) – this includes everything not in the categories below.
- A few items are subject to a *lower VAT rate* (5%), e.g. home energy supplies, supplies of energy to charitable non-business premises, sanitary protection and contraceptive products.
- Some items are *zero-rated for VAT* – VAT is charged as normal, but the rate is 0%. Products include books and other publications, children's clothing and cold food. VAT can still be reclaimed on purchases (for example, the paper to print the books, and so charities selling publications can often benefit from this). The 0% rate also applies to sales of donated goods (for example jumble sales and charity shops).
- Some sales are *VAT-exempt*, which means that you do not have to charge VAT on the sale but you cannot reclaim any corresponding VAT on purchases. VAT-exempt sales do not count towards the turnover in deciding whether you should be VAT registered. A number of charity services fall into this category, including educational services and welfare services provided by a 'relevant' charity (for definitions, see the publications on VAT under *Charities and tax issues* in *Further reading*). Fundraising events exempt from corporation tax are also classed as VAT-exempt (see *Charities and corporation tax*, page 150).
- Some income is classed as non-business income and is therefore *outside the scope of VAT*. This includes grants, donations and investment income.

The above list is only a very general summary – the full lists of zero-rated and VAT-exempt items take up many pages of legislation. Also, make sure you understand the crucial distinction between activities which are zero-rated and those which are VAT-exempt. Zero-rated sales are everyone's first choice in a charity: you do not have to add VAT to the sale price, but you can reclaim any VAT on related purchases. VAT-exempt sales are not so attractive – you do not have to add VAT to the sale price, but any VAT on the corresponding purchases will be irrecoverable.

Should our charity be VAT registered?

If your charity's total income is more than £70,000 (2010/11 figure), work out how much of this is trading income. This means being very clear whether funding agreements are grants or contracts (see *Understanding different funding channels*, page 142). Then deduct items that would be VAT-exempt (see above). If the total comes to more than about £60,000 you will need to watch the position carefully. If it goes over the threshold you must register for VAT within a month.

Note that *all* trading income – both primary purpose trading and trading for fundraising – counts for the VAT threshold.

Here are four examples.

- Charity A has a total income of £61,000. This is below the VAT threshold so, however the income is made up, it *does not* have to register.
- Charity B has a total income of £120,000, but £75,000 of this is from grants and donations. The remaining £45,000 is below the VAT threshold, so even if all of this was potentially VATable, it is below the threshold, so it *does not* have to register.
- Charity C is an educational organisation. Its total income is £90,000, of which £80,000 comes from course fees. Although this is trading income above the VAT threshold, the course fees would be VAT-exempt, so it *does not* have to register.
- Charity D has a total income of £100,000, of which £20,000 is from grants, donations and investments. The other £80,000 is trading income – half from publications sales and half from contracts for advice and consultancy services. All of the trading income is VATable (either zero rated or standard rated) and, as it totals more than £70,000, it *must register* immediately.

If you do this calculation and realise that your charity went over the VAT threshold some time ago, but you never registered, then a 'retrospective registration' will be needed. In other words, on the form VAT1, where you give the date from which the charity needs to be registered, this may be several years in the past. This can give rise to complex issues such as the need to re-invoice past work or, if this is not possible, previous income may have to be treated as VAT inclusive – which is a very expensive mistake.

For example, if for the last three years the charity had £75,000 of income from a home repairs service but had not registered for VAT, this £225,000 would be treated as a VAT-inclusive amount, and around £33,500 would have to be paid over to HMRC (less any VAT reclaimed on purchases). You would also have to submit retrospective VAT returns and the charity would be liable to VAT penalties unless the trustees could persuade HMRC they had a 'reasonable excuse' for not realising the position at the time. So you would almost certainly need specialist help.

However, in some cases, charities making a retrospective registration where they are able to re-invoice work (e.g. to a local authority) have found they are able to reclaim substantial VAT on past expenditure which more than covers the cost of the professional help. But a good charity treasurer should be monitoring the level of trading income and should never let his or her organisation get into this position.

Key terms

In any VAT publications you will find the following terms used.

* *Output VAT* – the VAT charged by the charity on goods or services you sell (if you are VAT registered).
* *Input VAT* – the VAT on the purchases made by the charity (this will be reclaimable if the charity is VAT registered but *only* when a purchase relates to an activity where VAT is charged on the income, so most charities end up with considerable amounts of irrecoverable input VAT).

Charities and corporation tax

Corporation tax is a tax on the trading profits of companies and other business organisations (this includes charities). For any trading activity you have to work out the profit, using the rule:

> Profit = Sales – Expenses

Even though the profit is only a surplus to be retained by the charity, in some cases it is subject to tax, otherwise charities would be able to run large commercial businesses on a tax-free basis, competing unfairly with other firms. In 2010/11, corporation tax is charged at 21% or 28% depending on the total profit. In working out the profit you can only deduct the expenses of the activity concerned (not the expenses of the whole charity), although you can include an element for the cost of voluntary time.

So, for example, a charity that runs a large successful coffee shop with relatively few expenses could find that, as well as having to charge VAT, a substantial slice of its income might have to be set aside for corporation tax. But there are ways round this, as described below.

Charity exemptions from corporation tax

The corporation tax rules contain a large number of charity exemptions, as follows. They are all subject to the condition that any profit is retained by the charity for the development of the service (but, in a charity, the trustees could not in any case benefit from a profit).

1   *Primary purpose trading.* Where the goods or services are provided directly as part of the charity's objects, there is no liability to corporation tax (though bear in mind that VAT could still apply). This is a very important rule. Some charities waste huge effort in setting up trading subsidiary companies when the activity they want to carry out is part of the charity's primary purpose.

    The liability to corporation tax only arises with trading for fundraising purposes. But even this has many exemptions, as summarised below.

2   *Where the trade is carried out mainly by the beneficiaries of the charity* – for example workshops run by blind people, coffee shops run mainly by people with learning disabilities or a car wash service run by young people. Although such income would be treated as a fundraising trade (rather than primary purpose) there is no corporation tax on any profit, provided that those doing the bulk of the work are the people whom the charity exists to support.

3   *Trades that are ancillary to the primary purpose* – for example accommodation for students or refreshments in an art gallery. These are also exempt from corporation tax. (However, if an art gallery runs a café which is open to the general public – not just those visiting the gallery – it would no longer satisfy the 'ancillary' test, unless you could show that the sales to non-gallery visitors were less than 10% of the total.)

4   *Any small-scale trading and fundraising activities within set limits* are also exempt. This rule, introduced from April 2000, is very flexible as,

within limits, it exempts *any* kind of trading for fundraising purposes from corporation tax. The vast majority of fundraising projects by small charities will fit this, even where the activity involves selling something. The condition is that the charity's total income (not the profit) from such activities is:

- not more than £5,000 in total; or
- not more than 25% of the charity's total income up to a maximum of £50,000 (for a charity with more than £200,000 income in total).

Table 11.4 gives examples.

Table 11.4 Small scale trading for fundraising – exemption from corporation tax

Charity's total income	Maximum trading income for fundraising that can escape corporation tax	
£3,000	£3,000	(Up to £5,000 allowed anyway)
£12,000	£5,000	(£5,000 allowed anyway)
£30,000	£7,500	(25% of income)
£160,000	£40,000	(25% of income)
£250,000	£50,000	(£50,000 upper limit)

But even when the trade is beyond those limits, there are further exemptions for certain types of trading income.

5   *Sales of donated goods* (for example jumble sales, charity shops, auctions of donated gifts) are exempt from corporation tax (and for VAT, the 0% rate applies).

6   There are also exemptions from corporation tax for *other specific fundraising events* (provided that they are supported because people know the event is for charity) in the cases of:

- small events of any kind, provided that the takings do not exceed £1,000 per week;
- larger events, provided that the charity holds no more than 15 events per year of the same type in any one location.

As well as the profits being exempt from corporation tax, the income from such activities counts as VAT-exempt. This means that you do not have to charge VAT on ticket sales for a fundraising event (but as a VAT-exempt activity you cannot then reclaim VAT costs related to the event, such as catering costs or equipment hire).

Trading outside the concessions – trading subsidiary companies

For most smaller charities, one or more of the above concessions will almost certainly cover your fundraising activities, and a liability to corporation tax is thus quite rare. But if you do go beyond these limits, it is up to the charity to make a corporation tax return to HMRC.

However, where a charity would end up paying a lot of corporation tax, a further solution is to set up a non-charitable trading subsidiary company (see figure 11.5 below). For example a charity that raised substantial funds through Christmas cards and catalogue sales could arrange for the scheme to be run by the subsidiary company rather than the charity itself. Although the company is liable to corporation tax on the profit, if it gives the whole of its profit back to the charity as a gift aid donation (see chapter 12), no corporation tax is paid.

Figure 11.5 A charity with a trading subsidiary

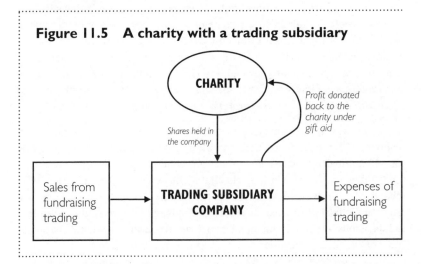

The subsidiary is then a separate entity – a social enterprise in its own right. So this means a lot of extra work; the trading subsidiary is a legally separate organisation: it is not itself a charity but a normal profit-making company. So it is usually established as a company limited by shares, with all the shares held by the charity (rather than as a company limited by guarantee as used for non-profit organisations). Some charities like to use the legal form of a CIC for a trading subsidiary to demonstrate that although it is trading commercially the trade is for a community purpose: to generate funds for the charity.

Because it is a legally separate body, the trading company needs completely separate accounts (both on a day-to-day basis, and separate year end accounts submitted to Companies House). It will need its own directors so that the charity and the subsidiary can enter into meaningful discussions and, of course, separate minutes must be kept for board meetings. (There may be some overlap with the charity trustees, but the Charity Commission recommends that there should always be at least one charity trustee who is not a director of the subsidiary, and at least one director of the subsidiary who is not a trustee of the charity.)

Because it is not a charity, the subsidiary will typically have to pay normal business rates if it occupies its own premises. Great care is also needed with regard to any expenses met by the charity that relate to the subsidiary. For example, if staff of the charity do work for the subsidiary, or if the charity lets the subsidiary occupy part of its premises, a written service agreement is needed with appropriate charges, otherwise the charity would be subsidising a commercial business. Moreover, it can be very difficult to deal with start-up costs for the company; the charity cannot give charitable funds to the subsidiary, so a commercial bank loan may be needed. Also, at year end, the charity may have to prepare group accounts, consolidating figures for the charity and the subsidiary – see *Charities with subsidiaries – group accounts* in chapter 7 (page 105).

However, any type of charity can, if necessary, have a trading subsidiary company. The subsidiary will almost always use the legal form of a company or CIC limited by shares, but the parent charity could be structured as a charitable trust, association, charitable incorporated organisation or a charitable company. In such cases people often get confused about the legal structures; part of the task of the treasurer is to make absolutely sure that all decisions, especially financial decisions, are clearly made in relation to the charity *or* the subsidiary – not fudged between the two.

Most large charities have a trading subsidiary – sometimes more than one – but since the concessions introduced in 2000 (see page 151), there are now very few cases where they are needed by smaller charities. There are one or two situations where a charity is undertaking a venture which is so risky that a separate company is felt to be needed purely to protect the charity, even though there is no saving of corporation tax (given that the trading subsidiary would have limited liability in its own right). But even so, if a charity's trading company failed, leaving bills unpaid, it is likely to cause serious damage to the charity's reputation. Running a separate subsidiary company means a major increase in the workload for the treasurer and finance staff, and only in the most exceptional cases is this justified for smaller charities.

Accounting for partnership arrangements

In recent years the government has placed huge emphasis on partnership working between the statutory and voluntary sectors, and has encouraged voluntary organisations themselves to work in partnership.

There are many arguments for and against partnerships, but it is vital that treasurers and finance officers are fully clear on the financial arrangements between partners, which can sometimes create major VAT liabilities (as well as other complications) if not handled correctly.

Figure 11.6   Example of a partnership arrangement

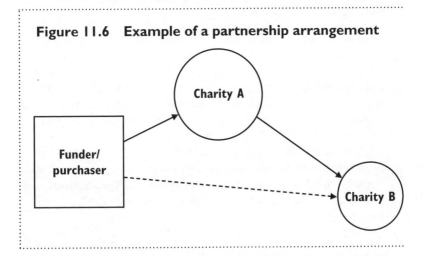

The main complications arise when two or more charities make a bid to undertake work on a joint basis. In most cases the funder will require one of the charities to act as the lead agency or 'accountable body' – taking overall responsibility for the work, and bringing in the other charity (or charities) as needed. Often the lead organisation will talk about 'sub-contracting' part of a project to a second charity – but this can be dangerous.

Suppose charity A is awarded £100,000 funding for a project, but charity B will handle part of the delivery (amounting to £40,000). There are several cases to consider.

- If the work is contract funded, and if A and B are both VAT registered charities, it is quite straightforward. B will invoice A for £40,000 + VAT, and A will invoice the original funder for £100,000 + VAT, reclaiming the VAT charged by B as part of its normal VAT return.

- If, however, the work is grant funded, problems can arise. If B is doing work for A under a sub-contract, then if B is VAT registered it *has* to charge VAT to A on the sub-contract work if B's work is for services which are standard rated and B is VAT registered. So B invoices A for £40,000 + 20% VAT = £48,000. Because the main work is grant funded, A cannot reclaim the VAT it has paid to B, and the grant is likely to be fixed at £100,000 in total. The net effect is that A is left with only £52,000 of the funding to carry out its own share of the work, rather than £60,000 as expected. (This scenario has created £8,000 of irrecoverable VAT, which is lost from charitable funding and transferred to the Exchequer.)

- It follows that, if the main work is grant funded, then *whether or not* A and B are VAT registered, it would be better for A to offer grant funding to B of £40,000 to carry out its share of the work. However, if this approach is to be used, it must be clear in all the paperwork from the outset – language such as 'sub-contracting' should be avoided. But, a grant agreement from A to B gives the trustees of A much less leverage over B if anything goes wrong, and the trustees of A must be confident that they can trust B to use the grant funding appropriately (they can, of course, require B to treat the grant as a restricted fund, but if the grant had conditions on services which B must supply to A, this could be challenged by HMRC that it was, in reality, a contract rather than a grant.)

- Another case – which can often be damaging for smaller charities seeking to work in partnerships – is if the work is contract funded and A is a large VAT registered charity but B is small organisation that is not VAT registered. B will thus invoice A for £40,000 (no VAT) and A will invoice the funder for £100,000 + VAT. However, because B is not VAT registered, it will have to bear the VAT cost on any purchases it makes – for example, if £12,000 of the £40,000 paid to B is for materials, this will incur £2,400 of VAT at 20%. If A prepared the initial funding bid, knowing the project would be carried out under a VATable contract but without knowing sub-contract arrangements at the time, A will probably have assumed that *all* VAT on purchases would be reclaimable. So A will typically insist that B has to do its share for £40,000. B will therefore, in effect, only have £37,600 to spend on what was budgeted as £40,000 of work (because £2,400 has gone on irrecoverable VAT). On the other hand, if A agreed to increase the payments to B, it could not then reclaim this extra cost as input VAT – because it is a charge from a non-VAT registered organisation – so A would then be left with only £57,600 (rather than £60,000) for its share. So, either way, £2,400 of the funding is lost as irrecoverable VAT. (The problem could be solved if B was willing to register for VAT voluntarily, but that may not be sensible if this is just a one-off short-term project. Alternatively, A and B could perhaps redraft the sub-contract arrangements so that all project materials were bought by A.)

- So if there would be VAT problems and if the funder will agree, it can be more attractive if A and B bid for the work as equal partners in terms of status, rather than one acting as a sub-contractor to the other. But unless there are two separate contracts (between the funder and A, and the funder and B), the two charities would be acting in partnership in the full legal sense and would then be considered 'jointly and severally liable' – i.e. A could be sued if B failed to deliver (or vice versa). Often trustees are unwilling to risk this.

So, apart from the first option where the work is funded by VATable contracts at all stages in the chain, irrecoverable VAT is likely to arise at some point, and it is important that whoever is preparing the initial bid allows for this in setting the project budgets. Alternatively, if A and B anticipate much partnership working on these lines, it may be worth considering a merger to form a single charity.

12 Linking fundraising and accounting

As this book has stressed throughout, the overall management of a charity's finances is a matter for the trustees as a whole. But implementation of the trustees' financial decisions normally falls to two key people or teams:

- the treasurer, together with the bookkeeper or finance officer; and
- the charity's main fundraiser (a trustee or a member of staff).

You may not use the term 'fundraiser', but there must always be someone who takes the lead on submitting grant applications, asking for donations, bidding for contracts or marketing the charity's services. Even if your charity is fortunate enough to have a regular stream of income from investments, those investments must be managed.

An accounting/fundraising team

Some charities also expect the treasurer to handle everything to do with fundraising – just because it relates to money. But this is normally too much for one person, and it is better to find ways of sharing responsibility.

Yet, sadly, in many charities – even in very small groups – there is often too little communication between the fundraiser and the person who handles the accounts – sometimes with disastrous results. This can be partly a matter of personality: fundraisers are often exuberant people who like to grasp opportunities and are frequently networking outside the confines of the charity, but they tend to find accounts rather boring. Treasurers and bookkeepers often have a quieter approach, with an emphasis on detail, and despair of getting others to follow clear procedures.

But unless a charity is successful in generating income, there will be no funds for which the treasurer has to account. On the other hand, fundraisers desperately need the charity to have good accounting procedures, so that once funds are received they are properly managed and used. There is nothing worse for a fundraiser than finding a donor or funder who makes a gift or a grant but who, when approached again, is reluctant to help because they were unhappy at how the first gift was accounted for or were not satisfied with the charity's published accounts.

Here is a checklist of possible areas where you need to work out effective communication and division of responsibilities.

- *Issuing receipts for gifts* – who is responsible? Who writes the acknowledgement letter? With a large-scale appeal, the response handling and accounting for gifts may be the biggest task.

- *Purpose of gifts* – is there a simple mechanism to ensure the treasurer or bookkeeper knows to which fund every grant or donation relates?

- *New restricted funds* – is the fundraiser authorised to invent new projects (which would mean new restricted funds) or must this be approved by others? How does the treasurer or bookkeeper know when to create a new fund in the books?

- *Costing of new projects* – when bidding for funds, who works out what to ask for? And if you do not get all you ask for, who decides whether to continue or whether to drop the project?

- *Deciding when to refuse a gift.*

- *Pledges verses actual gifts* – once you have a promise of support, who is responsible for contacting the donor or funder to ensure that the gifts are received? Sometimes a fundraiser feels that an appeal is complete when the target is reached. But it may need four or five years of accounting for regular donations (and issuing reminders where needed) before all the funds are in the bank.

- *Banking of income* – who does what, especially with fundraising events? Is the treasurer expected to have people calling unexpectedly with bags of cash? Or are those who organise cash collections responsible for counting and banking the proceeds? (Remember the need for controls – see chapter 6.)

- *Cash floats* – if you are running a stall of any kind, what is the procedure for drawing and accounting for cash floats?

- *Showing income on the statement of financial activities (SOFA)* (see chapter 7) – when money comes in from fundraising events, are the trading and donated income distinguished (see chapter 4 for the principles)? If not, how can you get a sensible estimate of the split?

- *Fundraising expenses* – fundraisers need to keep a note of the costs of fundraising activities run by the charity so they can be included correctly in the accounts. Under the Statement of Recommended Practice (SORP), you cannot just show the net income.

- *Paying advance fundraising costs* – if a fundraising activity needs payment up front, for example to hire a venue or print brochures, who approves this? What about cashflow (see chapter 9)?
- *Gift aid tax claims* – if you have donations from individuals, it will usually be possible to reclaim tax under gift aid (see *Gift aid*, below). Who will manage this? Who is responsible for getting gift aid declarations completed? Who signs the tax claim submitted to HM Revenue & Customs (HMRC)? And if the claim covers gifts for different funds, do you know how to split the tax recovered?
- *Fundraising database* – if you have more than about 20 donors you will probably need a donor database of some kind, to keep track of who has given what, and this will probably link to the gift aid procedures. Who is responsible for this? If the fundraiser, is he or she aware of the need for auditability of the information (by both the charity's auditor/ independent examiner and by HMRC)?
- *Incoming standing orders* – if you have donors making regular gifts by bankers order, who checks the bank statement against the donors' pledges? (It is generally best if the statement first goes to the person who records gifts into the fundraising database, and then to the treasurer with a total for the main books. If this is cumbersome, consider having a separate bank account for incoming standing orders.)
- *Direct debits* are still rare on the income side in smaller charities due to the processes and bank assurances required, but the big difference from standing orders is that direct debits must be requested each month (or as agreed) by the charity. You will almost certainly have an automated system agreed with your bank or an agency – but who is responsible for this system at the charity's end? In particular, what is the procedure for refunds in the event of errors or donor complaints?
- *Credit/debit card gifts* – more local charities are starting to accept these. Who is responsible for the procedures?
- *Charities Aid Foundation (CAF) and similar cheques* – CAF has schemes where donors pay into a CAF account on which tax is reclaimed, and the donors can direct funds to any charity of their choice by writing a CAF cheque. But once received by the charity, the cheques must be sent off to CAF, which will pay the funds into your bank. Who handles this? Do you have a means to ensure such gifts are not erroneously treated as gift aid? (Some other agency charities have similar schemes.)
- *VAT* – where goods are sold for fundraising purposes, VAT may be applicable (see chapter 11). Who is responsible for establishing the VAT position and setting prices to allow for this?

- *Funders requiring invoices* – for work done under contracts, the charity will have to invoice the funder: who is responsible? If the amount varies, who is responsible for the invoice figure? Are you clear on the VAT issues (see chapter 11)? If someone other than the treasurer raises invoices, does the treasurer know about unpaid invoices in order to include them as debtors at year end?

- *Loan finance* – sometimes a major project will require the charity to take on a loan to cover initial costs for a new service or a major fixed asset such as a new building. Naturally this will need detailed discussion by trustees, but even if agreed in principle there is much work in applying for a loan – is raising loan finance the responsibility of the fundraiser or the treasurer? Moreover, loans are usually subject to interest – remember to allow for the interest payments (not just the capital repayments) in fundraising plans and project budgets.

- *Subsidiary groups* – how do all these procedures work if the charity has subsidiary groups managing their own books (see chapter 6)? This is especially important with semi-independent fundraising teams – if their events are run on behalf of the charity, both their income and their expenses must appear in the charity's accounts. Or are they independent groups that raise funds and simply pass them on to you as donations?

There are not many charities where fewer than four or five of these issues apply. If you have established a good relationship, with plenty of communication, between yourself and those who bring in the funds, it will make your job much easier and will greatly improve the overall financial management of the charity.

The rest of this chapter addresses some of the above areas.

Gift aid

Gift aid is the government scheme whereby a UK taxpayer gives to charity, and the charity can reclaim the income tax paid by the donor on his or her gift.

Some charities get much of their income through gift aid donations, and thus receive a great deal of government support for their work. The big attraction is that gift aid applies to *any* organisation with charitable status.

Regardless of the donor's personal tax rate, the gift is treated as being made net of basic rate income tax. So to work out how much tax you can reclaim, you have to *gross up* the gift. With income tax at 20% from April 2008 this means you get an extra 25% on all donations made under gift aid (this is less than in the past, but still worthwhile, and until 2010/11 the government is paying a further 3.2% supplement). For example:

- Sue Brown earns £100. Assuming she pays tax at 20% basic rate, £20 tax is deducted and she will receive £80 after tax.
- If she gives the £80 to charity, and completes a gift aid declaration, the charity can reclaim the £20 tax she has paid. So in total, the charity gets £100.
- By completing a gift aid declaration, Sue has enabled the charity to gain £20 tax on top of her £80 gift. As £20 represents 25% of £80, the value of her gift to the charity is increased by 25%.

  (In fact, until 2010/11, the charity will actually get £22.56 back from HMRC: the £20 tax paid by Sue and £2.56 transitional gift aid relief.)

The conditions to reclaim tax are shown below.

Table 12.1   Conditions for a reclaiming tax on a donation under the gift aid scheme

1. It must be a genuine donation from an identifiable individual donor made out of their post-tax income:
   - not a payment for goods or services;
   - not a donation from a business.

2. The recipient must be a charity in UK tax law (this includes exempt or excepted charities). From 2010 it can even include organisations in other EU countries if they meet the UK tax definition of a charity.

3. Payment must actually be made and evidence of this must be available (i.e. an audit trail of money received).

4. The donor must be a UK taxpayer (income tax or capital gains tax).
   - The donor must pay enough tax in total to cover the tax being reclaimed by the charity (but donor's tax rate does not matter).

5. The donor must make a *declaration* that he/she wishes the gift to be treated as gift aid.
   - The gift aid declaration must cover all issues required by the regulations – but it can be open-ended to cover all future gifts. You do not have to use specific forms, and with the required procedures you can also accept declarations by telephone or Internet.

6. The donor must not get any but the most trivial benefit from the gift – i.e. it must be a genuine donation. If you are considering giving the donor anything in return, e.g. free tickets for an event, or some item of value, be sure you understand the rules. The limit on any benefits to the donor are as follows (and if the donor makes several gifts in a year, the rules are based on the total of all gifts made):
   - for small gifts up to £100 the maximum benefit is 25% of the of net gift;
   - from £100 to £1,000 the maximum benefit is £25;
   - from £1,000 to £10,000 the maximum benefit is 5% of the net gift;
   - for gifts over £10,000, the maximum benefit is £500.

7. The charity must publish annual accounts and make them available to HMRC (and anyone else) on request.

8. The charity must be willing to have its books and records for gift aid donations subject to HMRC audit (this includes bank statements, gift aid declarations and fundraising literature, as well as gift aid books and systems).

Once you have set up a gift aid scheme, it is worth including even quite small donations because it adds very little extra work, and with regular gifts the amounts build up. If someone gives £5 a month, this is £60 a year, and you will reclaim £15 in tax. With 70 supporters giving at this level, you will add more than £1,000 a year in tax reclaims. You can apply gift aid to membership subscriptions, provided that the subscription is largely a donation, where any benefits to the member have little financial value – see the rules above (and where different members receive different benefits, special rules apply). However, gift aid only applies to identified donors – not to loose cash in collecting tins and plates.

In the case of charities which charge for admission to a property, museum, gallery, nature reserve or similar, gift aid is permitted on the amount paid (even though the donor gets the benefit of admission) provided that they *either* pay at least 10% more than the normal price, *or* if they are buying an annual season ticket. (There are detailed HMRC rules governing how these issues are measured.) Bear in mind that even though gift aid is allowed, a payment for admission will count as trading income and may be subject to VAT (see chapter 11).

You need to take care, however, to ensure that gift aid declarations are properly worded to reflect the rules, as set out in the HMRC guidance (see figure 12.2). Many charities have launched appeals with donation forms where the gift aid declaration is invalid. Also you must have sufficient information to identify the donor – the absolute minimum is a surname, initial, postcode and house number and the address must be the *home* address. You do not need to use the exact form of words shown in the figure, neither do you have to give all the options, but inclusion of the note shown in bold at the end (or words to that effect) is a legal requirement. If you use the third option (where the declaration covers past and future gifts), note that a donor cannot backdate the declaration by more than six tax years (for many years charities used declarations covering all gifts since 6 April 2000 – but this is now more than six years. A declaration made in the tax year 2010/11, for example, cannot be backdated earlier than 6 April 2004).

Claims for repayment of tax are made to HMRC Charities at Bootle, using form R68 Claim and a schedule of the gift aid donations on form R68 Gift Aid (or a schedule giving the same information – see figure 12.3 for an example). From 2008/09, the claim should be made at 20% tax, and HMRC will pay the additional transitional supplement when applicable. Claims for gifts made in different tax years must be submitted separately, but it is possible to make several claims per year, provided that you are claiming at least £100 of tax on each occasion (charities below this are asked to claim just once a year).

Figure 12.2 Sample gift aid declaration

Name of charity ....

Details of donor

Title .... Forename(s) .... Surname ....

Address ....

....

.... Postcode ....

I want the charity to treat
* the enclosed donation of £ ....

* the donation(s) of £ .... which I made on ..../....../.......

* all donations I have made for this tax year and the six years prior to the
year of this declaration and all donations I make from the date of this
declaration until I notify you otherwise
as gift aid donations.

* delete as appropriate

Date ...../...../.....

**You must pay an amount of income tax and/or capital gains tax at least
equal to the tax the charity reclaims on your donations in the appropriate
tax year (currently 25p for each £1 you give).**

Source: www.hmrc.gov.uk

Efficient systems and procedures are vital. You need someone methodical
in charge of the scheme (and with a good respect for donor confidentiality).
Moreover, HMRC now requires that claims must be made by a trustee or
member of staff who is 'fit and proper' – this is because some people have
tried to establish bogus charities in order to reclaim gift aid, or have
abused legitimate charities for the same purpose.

The process can be done manually, but computer-based systems are
available to help with this – often linked with other fundraising database
facilities to facilitate communication with supporters and maintain a
history of each donor's contributions over many years.

A key role of such systems is to automate the preparation of tax claims, and to
assist with the long-term records needed for HMRC audits (particularly
important if you have donors giving regularly, where several weekly or
monthly gifts may be combined for a claim). Larger charities may use a
fundraising database integrated with their accounting system. However, if

you want to record one-off gifts and work out the tax reclaimable, you may find that a spreadsheet is sufficient – HMRC will accept tax claims prepared in spreadsheets provided that they contain all the required information.

Your trustees need to be aware that HMRC normally pays tax claims as submitted but retains the right to inspect your books, and if problems are found on a gift aid audit, the charity could have to repay large amounts of tax reclaimed. On average, a charity claiming gift aid will have an HMRC audit roughly every three years, but the frequency can vary enormously – charities perceived as 'low risk' may go for a very long time without an audit. So it is crucial to ensure that gift aid declarations are well stored. If you have an audit, HMRC will typically choose a small sample of gifts to review in detail, but if you can only produce (say) 92% of the gift aid declaration for this sample, HMRC may assume that only 92% of tax was validly reclaimed, and hence the charity could be required to repay 8% of all the tax reclaimed for the last six years (though from 2008 you should be given a chance to remedy the situation before any penalty is imposed, and small levels of errors will be overlooked). People often remain loyal to charities for decades, and a gift aid declaration completed in 2001 could in theory still be needed in 2050 – although HMRC is considering a rule under which declarations would only have to be kept for six years.

Further changes to gift aid procedures are expected in the coming years (especially from April 2011 when the repayment supplement ends). The website www.direct.gov.uk/giftaid should provide the latest information.

Figure 12.3 Example of a gift aid tax claim to HMRC (R68 Gift Aid substitute)

MIDSHAM COMMUNITY ASSOCIATION – GIFT AID TAX CLAIM   13 July 2010

SCHEDULE OF GIFT AID DONATIONS   Reference: X999999Y

Tax year 10/11   Amounts in £

Name of donor	Date of last donation	Amounts given	Reference
Peter Bloggs	18 May 10	40.00	1
Hugh Bone	27 Apr 10	400.00	12
Jane Brown	27 Apr 10	100.00	8
Joanna Jenkins	27 Apr 10	25.00	11
Susannah Jones	18 May 10	7.00	2
Philip Thomson-Giles	18 May 10	45.00	13
Rowena Whitely	18 May 10	10.00	10

No of donors: 7	Total given:	627.00	
	Tax reclaimable:	156.75 at 20.00%	

If your charity has not previously operated gift aid, contact HMRC Charities with details of your charity registration number (Charity Commission, OSCR or CCNI) if applicable and the date of your accounting year (for charities in England and Wales excepted from registration, HMRC will also need further details). Provided that your charitable status is clear, and that claims will be made by a 'fit and proper' person, HMRC should allocate you a charity reference (do not confuse this with your registered charity number) and you can then start making gift aid claims.

Gift aid means that any charity that is able to generate gifts from individuals can get further help from the government. But to operate it effectively needs careful coordination between fundraisers and treasurers.

In addition to the tax reclaimed by the charity, donors who pay higher rates of tax (40% or 50%) can get further tax relief, so if you are seeking substantial donations it is worth bearing in mind these rules. For example, in 2010/11 a donor could give £1 million to charity but the cost to them (after tax relief) would be only £484,500 once you allow for the donor paying tax at 50% and the charity reclaiming gift aid supplement. However, the rules on higher rate relief may change after 2011.

Fundraising ethics

A charity's reputation can easily be ruined by inappropriate forms of fundraising, and unless there is a specific trustee with oversight of fundraising, the treasurer will often have a key role in this. For example, the treasurer or finance officer should certainly be involved in approval of literature where donors are promised that their gifts will be used in a specific way, to ensure that systems are in place to track such gifts and allocate them to the correct restricted funds.

The Charities Act 2006 includes provisions to allow the government to regulate fundraising of any kind. However, the government is keen to encourage a self-regulatory approach, and has supported the creation of the Fundraising Standards Board (FRSB) (see *Useful addresses*) under which charities sign up to a 'Fundraising Promise'. This makes various commitments to donors and funders, including an agreement by the charity to abide by FRSB rulings in the event of complaints about the charity's fundraising (though complaints must be raised with the charity first).

The FRSB works on a membership basis with an annual subscription from charities that sign up to the scheme, but the fees are on a sliding scale so that even the smallest charities can afford to join. The only charities unaffected by this are those whose income comes *solely* from primary purpose trading or from investments.

The Codes of Fundraising Practice published by the Institute of Fundraising (see *Useful addresses*) provide clear guidance on what is or is not appropriate in relation to many forms of fundraising, and these form the basis of the FRSB's expected standards. The Codes also provide guidance on issues such as the acceptance and refusal of donations and payment of fundraisers on a commission basis, as well as matters such as safety and respect for the environment in fundraising events.

Whilst a treasurer will rarely be a fundraising expert, the crucial links between fundraising and accounting mean that treasurers need to be aware of these Codes, and treasurers will often be more aware than other trustees of the impact of regulation – and hence of the benefits of a self-regulatory scheme such as the FRSB.

Investments

For charities which have significant investments, the arrangements for investment management are crucial if the charity is to have the income needed and is to be able to sustain its work for future years. Although investment management is not usually seen as part of fundraising, costs of investment management are classified by SORP 2005 as part of the 'Cost of generating funds' on the SOFA and income from investments is classed as 'Generated income'.

Investment management for charities is a major issue beyond the scope of this book. However, there are various firms of investment managers with special experience of work with charities who are able to provide expert help. (In fact, this is an area where trustees *must* take professional advice if they do not have the relevant expertise themselves.)

The involvement of the treasurer and/or finance officer in investment decisions will vary considerably between charities, but if the trustees have an investments subcommittee, the treasurer will usually be a member and will often play a leading role when decisions are taken from time to time on the appointment of investment managers.

The treasurer and finance officer also need to be active in helping the trustees to agree an 'investment policy' – for example, in clarifying timescales for holding investments in relation to the various funds of the charity, the levels of income needed and the relative importance of income and capital growth. Also, many charities now have an ethical investment policy, to ensure that the charity only invests in companies whose work does not conflict with the charity's objects. Such policies must be stated in the trustees' annual report (see table 7.1).

Costing projects and fundraising bids, and refusing gifts

Not all offers of money are helpful to a charity. Donations subject to very tight restrictions may be simply too much work to justify a restricted fund for one specific gift. Also, some restrictions might break your own policies or even be illegal. For example, few charities would feel it right to accept gifts with conditions on the race of beneficiaries, unless it was a project addressing specific racial disadvantage.

Just as damaging are offers of funds that require the charity to do something but do not cover the full costs, including relevant overheads and management time (see *Managing core costs: full cost recovery* in chapter 4, page 48). Sometimes the trustees will feel that the project is sufficiently central to their objects to justify subsidising it with a contribution from general funds. But very often treasurers find out too late that someone has committed the charity to a new project that had not been properly costed, and which will prove a net drain on the charity's general funds.

Issues of costing and budgeting have been addressed in several chapters. The time to work out costs is when a new project is first being considered, and this needs close liaison between the fundraiser and treasurer or finance officer to ensure everything is included. It is all too easy to forget the VAT, the professional fees, the employer's national insurance (NI), the cost of salary increments over the life of the project, the recruitment costs, the premises overheads, the maintenance and annual depreciation of capital items, the increase in accountancy costs, the management time to supervise a project, and all the other elements involved.

If you tell a funder, 'We need £40,000 to do this', you may get what you ask for. Even if you do not, you have only lost the cost of the time spent on the proposal. But if you say you can do it for £30,000, get the go ahead and then come back asking for more money, most funders are likely to refuse and will also regard the charity as less than competent when it comes to future requests. The lower bid may succeed, but at a net cost to the charity of £10,000. If the funder could really only find £30,000 it would be better to refuse to do the project (or to propose something smaller where £30,000 would cover everything).

Charity finance as a whole

In this book we have looked at a vast range of financial issues, from basic bookkeeping to the legal requirements for charity accounts, to issues of charity tax, and implications for fundraising. You will have seen how these issues need to be considered as a whole, and the idea that a treasurer or finance officer is just someone who 'keeps the books' does not make any sense, even in the smallest charity.

In order to make this a 'handbook' that can be read in a few hours, there are many topics only mentioned in passing, and if such issues affect your charity, you will need to refer to further sources or seek professional guidance. Also, the field of charity finance is constantly developing, with new legislation, new versions of the SORP, changing tax rules and new initiatives in government policies towards the third sector. But if you have a good general understanding of the topics covered here, you will be very well placed to support your charity in its management of finance.

Being an effective charity treasurer or finance officer is partly about good accounting procedures, and partly about understanding the legal requirements, so that you can advise and support your trustees. But it is also about recognising the privilege of managing monies that are not your own, which have been given to your charity in the hope of making the world a better place. If, by taking on the finance role, you can enable your charity's funds to be used effectively for the cause set out in its objects, you will be making a major contribution to society.

Appendix: Differences for accounting years that began prior to April 2010 and future changes known

In this book the various legal requirements for charity accounting are based on the rules that apply as of 1 June 2010. However, in the years leading up to this, a number of changes to the rules occurred which will be relevant if you are involved in producing accounts for earlier years. Some changes which do not take effect until 2011 or later are known in advance and are also covered here.

This appendix summarises the main differences. It is written in date order, explaining changes as they took effect, starting from the introduction of SORP 2005 in April 2005 as it is easiest to understand the changes in chronological order. However, depending on the year you are working on, you may find it easiest to start from the final accounting changes in this appendix and then work back to see which other changes may not have taken effect for the year you are considering.

Because accounts cover a period of time – normally a year – any legal changes have to relate to a certain point in the year, and the normal rule is that new legal changes relate to accounting years which *start on or after* the date specified. (Strictly speaking the rules refer to "accounting periods" because occasionally a charity will have an accounting period which is longer or shorter than 12 months.)

So, for example, in the case of the changes listed here as effective from 1 April 2008, they can be applied for a set of charity accounts for an accounting year 1 April 2008 – 31 March 2009 or later. But if your charity works on a calendar accounting year (31 December year end) you *could not* apply the April 2008 changes to your 2008 accounting year because it began on 1 January 2008, i.e. before 1 April 2008. So, in this case, your year ending 31 December 2009 accounting would be the first when you could take advantages of the changes implemented from 1 April 2008.

1 April 2005

- Implementation of the *SORP 2005* standard (replacing SORP 2000) – this applies to charities throughout the UK if preparing accounts on an accruals basis. (However, in this case, 'early adoption was encouraged' so a charity could apply SORP 2005 for a year which began before 1 April 2005 if the trustees had not approved the relevant accounts by the time SORP 2005 was issued.)

- In England and Wales, the *Charities (Accounts and Reports) Regulations 2005* replaced the former regulations from 1995 and 2000 and made many provisions of SORP 2005 a legal requirement for non-company charities preparing accounts on the accruals basis.
- New rules in England and Wales for audit and independent examination of NHS charities.

14 July 2005

- Royal Assent for *Charities and Trustee Investment (Scotland) Act 2005* – but no immediate effect on accounting issues until April 2006.

1 April 2006

- Implementation of the *Charities Accounts (Scotland) Regulations 2006* – replacing the former Charities Accounts (Scotland) Regulations 1992. For accounting years from this date, Scottish charities must follow the rules stated in this book for preparation of accounts (receipts and payments accounts allowed up to £100,000 income, accruals above this). Accounts can be independently examined up to £500,000 income (or £2.8 million assets). New reporting duties for independent examiners, closer to those for England and Wales. (Previously, under the 1992 Regulations, receipts and payments accounts were only allowed up to £25,000 income, and independent examination was only allowed up to £100,000 income.)

9 November 2006

- Royal Assent for *Charities Act 2006* – but no immediate impact on accounting issues until February 2007.
- Royal Assent for *Companies Act 2006* – but no immediate impact on accounting issues until April 2008.

24 February 2007

- From this date it became compulsory for UK-wide charities regularly using premises in Scotland (see chapter 1) to register with OSCR in order to be allowed to refer to themselves as 'charities' in Scotland. Once registered with OSCR – even if also registered with the Charity Commission – the charity's accounts must comply with the Charities Accounts (Scotland) Regulations 2006 which, in most respects, are more strict than the rules for England and Wales.

27 February 2007

First changes under Charities Act 2006 took effect as follows.

- Independent examination threshold increased from £250,000 to £500,000 income for non-company charities in England and Wales – subject to requirement for the independent examiner to hold a professional qualification for this new band (see chapter 8 for details).
- Reporting accountant threshold for charitable companies in England, Wales and Scotland increased from £250,000 to £500,000 income (pending more substantial changes from April 2008 to replace the reporting accountant regime with independent examination of charitable companies).
- New £2.8 million assets threshold for audit now applies for most charities (even if the income is below £500,000) – see chapter 8 for details.
- Rules in England and Wales now based on total income for the year concerned (no need to consider expenditure if larger than income). Also no need from this date to consider income in previous years when considering if audit is required. (For years which began prior to 27 February 2007, an audit could be triggered if the income or expenditure was over £250,000 for the current year or either of the two previous years).
- Various other changes implemented under Charities Act 2006 – mainly related to powers of the Charity Commission.

23 April 2007

- Compulsory registration threshold for charities in England and Wales increased to £5,000 income unless the charity is excepted or exempt. (Previously the limit in most cases was £1,000).

1 April 2008

- New definition of 'charity' took effect in England and Wales under Charities Act 2006 – see chapter 1.
- Reporting accountant provisions for charitable companies are replaced by independent examination, with same thresholds as for non-company charities (so, in England and Wales, a charitable company must have an independent examination if its income is over £10,000; for charities registered in Scotland there is no lower limit). This change resulted from orders under the Companies Act 2006 *and* Charities Act 2006. (Prior to this, a completely separate 'reporting accountant' regime applied under company law for charitable companies with income in range £90,000 to £500,000 – or £90,000 to £250,000 for years prior to 27 February 2007. This covered much less than an independent examination, but the reporting accountant had to be a member of one of the specified professional bodies for this purpose.)

- *Charities (Accounts and Reports) Regulations 2008* take effect in England and Wales (replacing the 2005 Regulations).
- Legal requirements for group accounts take effect: from April 2008 a charity with a subsidiary *must* prepare group accounts if the group income is over £500,000 net, or £600,000 gross (i.e. before eliminating transfers between the subsidiary and the parent charity) – such accounts will necessarily be subject to audit. (See *Charities with subsidiaries–group accounts* in chapter 7, page 105.)
- New rules on trustees' annual reports in England and Wales regarding public benefit. The trustees' report must now include statements on how the charity has advanced its purposes for the public benefit and on whether or not the trustees have 'had regard' to the Charity Commission's guidance on this (see *What about the annual report?* in chapter 7).
- New whistle-blowing duties for charity auditors and independent examiners.
- Deadline for charities registered with OSCR to make this clear on all literature (even if also registered with the Charity Commission).

May 2008

- Second edition of SORP 2005 issued, with an additional introduction clarifying the issues for smaller charities (but the standard itself, SORP 2005, is unaffected).

9 September 2008

- Royal assent for Charities Act (Northern Ireland) 2008 – but no immediate impact.

31 January 2009

- Compulsory registration begins for formerly excepted and exempted charities in England and Wales where income is over £100,000. This threshold is due to reduce over time, but not before late 2011.

27 March 2009

- Charity Commission for Northern Ireland (CCNI) came into being under Charities Act (Northern Ireland) 2008 with associated powers.

1 April 2009

- Accounting thresholds in England and Wales increased. Lower income limit for compulsory independent examinations (and compulsory filing of accounts for charities registered with the Charity Commission) increased to £25,000 (previously £10,000). Receipts and payments accounts permitted for non-company charities up to £250,000 income (previously £100,000). Asset threshold at which audit becomes compulsory increased to £3.26 million (previously £2.8 million) – though this now only affects charities in the £250,000 to £500,000 income range. These changes (unusually) apply to years *ending* on or after 1 April 2009 (so they cannot be used for years ending 31

March 2009, but a charity preparing accounts based on the tax year could use the new thresholds for the year ending 5 April 2009.)

25 September 2009

- New definition of 'charity' and associated public benefit requirement took effect under Charities Act (Northern Ireland) 2008.

8 April 2010

- The CCNI has taken over the list of Northern Irish charities held by HMRC. However further regulations are needed for CCNI to start registrations of new charities in Northern Ireland (expected late 2010).

1 June 2010

- First stage of formerly exempt charities in England and Wales losing their exempt status. Some (such as English universities) come under new 'Principal Regulators' – others (such as Oxbridge colleges and students' unions and Welsh universities) have to apply for charity registration if over £100,000 income.

4 January 2011

- Standard rate of VAT increases from 17.5% to 20%

Early 2011

- Likely first registration for charitable incorporated organisations (CIOs) in England and Wales (provisional date not confirmed at time of going to press). First registrations of SCIOs likely to follow a few months later followed by CIOs in Northern Ireland.

1 April 2011

- Accounting thresholds for charities registered in Scotland increase. Receipts and payments accounts to be allowed for non-company charities below £250,000 income (previously £100,000) and the asset threshold for audit goes up to £3.26 million (previously £2.8 million). (Unlike the changes in England and Wales on 1 April 2009, this change is *not* expected to be backdated, so it is due to take effect only for years ending 31 March 2012 onwards.)
- Likely start of accounting regulations for charities registered in Northern Ireland. (The regulations may not be finalised until around October 2011, but they are likely to apply to accounting years starting from 1 April 2011.)

June 2011

- Likely second stage for exempt charities in England and Wales to have to start registering with the Charity Commission if over £100,000 income (unless covered by

Principal Regulators). This is expected to include industrial and provident societies recognised as charities.

2012

- Possible reduction in the £100,000 threshold for registration of excepted charities in England and Wales (churches etc).
- Possible start of registration with CCNI of charities based elsewhere but operating in Northern Ireland (section 167 registrations under the Charities Act (Northern Ireland) 2008).

Further reading

Charity Commission publications

The Charity Commission produces a wide range of guidance booklets for charities. The more important ones are produced in printed form, but many are now only available from the Commission's website. In almost all cases they apply to excepted charities in England and Wales as well as registered charities. (See *Useful addresses* for contact information.)

The following are particularly relevant to treasurers and finance workers.

CC3   – *The Essential Trustee*

CC8   – *Internal Financial Controls for Charities*

CC11   – *Trustee Expenses and Payments*

CC14   – *Investment of Charitable Funds: Basic Principles*

CC15b – *Charity Reporting and Accounting: The Essentials* April 2009

CC16   – *Receipts and Payments Accounts Pack*

CC17   – *Accruals Accounts Pack*

CC19   – *Charities' Reserves*

CC31   – *Independent Examination of Charity Accounts: Trustees' Guide*

CC32   – *Independent Examination of Charity Accounts: Examiners' Guide*

CC35   – *Trustees, Trading and Tax*

CC60   – *The Hallmarks of a Well-Run Charity*

Accounting and Reporting by Charities: Statement of Recommended Practice (SORP 2005) (2nd edn 2008) (This is also available in printed form, published by CCH Publications – see below under *Accounting standards*)

Any treasurer of a charity whose income is more than £250,000 should certainly have a copy of the full SORP. For smaller charities, the simplified guidance in CC16 or CC17, together with the principles explained in this book, may be sufficient.

Publications from the Office of the Scottish Charity Regulator (OSCR)

Many of the principles in Charity Commission publications (if not the legal details) are also relevant in Scotland. However, OSCR has produced the following introductory booklets (available in print and from OSCR's website) specifically on the Scottish charity accounting requirements. (See *Useful addresses* for contact information.)

Scottish Charity Accounts – A Brief Guide

Scottish Charity Accounts – Part 1: The Overview

Scottish Charity Accounts – Part 2: Receipts and Payments Accounts

Scottish Charity Accounts – Part 3: Fully Accrued Accounts

OSCR Receipts and Payments Accounting Workpack

Independent Examination: OSCR Guidance for Charities and Independent Examiners

Books on preparing published charity accounts

Charities: An Industry Accounting and Auditing Guide (4th edn), David Chitty and Nick Morgan, Croner CCH, 2006

Charity Accounts: A Practical Guide to the Charities SORP (4th edn), Andrew Pianca and Greyham Dawes, Jordans, 2010

A Practical Guide to Charity Accounting, Kate Sayer, Directory of Social Change, 2003 (Note: This pre-dates SORP 2005 although a new edition is expected)

Legislation on charity accounts

ACTS

Charities Act 1993

Charities Act 2006

Charities and Trustee Investment (Scotland) Act 2005

Charities Act (Northern Ireland) 2008

STATUTORY INSTRUMENTS

Charities (Accounts and Reports) Regulations 2008 (SI 2008/629)

Charities Accounts (Scotland) Regulations 2006 (SSI 2006/218)

Note: All legislation is available to purchase from bookshops or can be accessed free online from the Office of Public Sector Information (www.opsi.gov.uk). However, published versions (whether in print or online) will refer to the legislation *as originally enacted*. In particular, the Charities Act 1993 was amended by various other pieces of legislation after 1993 but prior to the major changes made by the Charities Act 2006. Legislation as amended is becoming available from www.statutelaw.gov.uk; however, it is important to check the tables provided on this site for amendments not yet incorporated. A new consolidated Charities Act for England and Wales is expected in 2010/11 but this is for ease of reading and is not expected to change any issues of substance.

Accounting standards

Accounting and Reporting by Charities: Statement of Recommended Practice, March 2005 (SORP 2005) (2nd edn May 2008) CCH Publications (Also available online from the Charity Commission)

Financial Reporting Standard for Smaller Entities (FRSSE), Accounting Standards Board April 2008, FRC Publications (Also available online from www.frc.org.uk)

There are also a number of documents that amplify the SORP in relation to particular types of charities, for example:

The Charities Act 1993 and the PCC (3rd edn), Church House Publishing 2005 (Covers specific issues for Church of England Parochial Church Councils – PCCs)

SORP Made Simpler: Guidance for Grant-making Charities Reporting Under the Charities SORP 2005, John Shuffrey, ACF 2006

Books on charity financial management

Income to Impact: Financial Stewardship of Public Sector and Not-for-profit Organisations, Adrian Poffley, Directory of Social Change 2010

Full Cost Recovery: A Guide and Toolkit on Cost Allocation – Version II, ACEVO 2010

The Good Financial Management Guide for the Voluntary Sector, Paul Palmer, National Council for Voluntary Organisations (NCVO) Publications 2005

Introductory Pack on Funding and Finance for Voluntary and Community Organisations (6 vols), Deborah Turton ed., NCVO/Finance Hub 2006, free but postage charged for printed copies

A Practical Guide to Financial Management for Charities and Voluntary Organisations (3rd edn), Kate Sayer, Directory of Social Change 2007

Charities and tax issues

Charity Accounting and Taxation (5th edn), The Buzzacott Charity Team, Bloomsbury Professional 2010

Charity Taxation: A Definitive Handbook, Adrian Randall and Stephen Williams, Jordans 2001

A Practical Guide to VAT for Charities and Voluntary Organisations (3rd edn), Kate Sayer, Directory of Social Change 2007

Value Added Tax – Charities, HM Revenue & Customs VAT Notice 701/1
(Summarises the main VAT rules specific to charities, through various supplementary notices may also be applicable)

VAT for Voluntary Organisations (6th edn), Graham Elliott, NCVO Publications 2005

Investments

The Good Investment Guide for the Voluntary Sector, Catherine Wood, NCVO Publications 2007

Charity law

The Charities Act 2006: A Guide for Foundations and Grant-making Trusts in England and Wales, Gareth G Morgan, ACF 2007
Although this guide pays special attention to issues for grantmakers, it covers all the main areas of the Act and is thus relevant to charities of all kinds

Charities Act 2006 – What Trustees Need to Know, Cabinet Office/Charity Commission 2007, free (but printed copies only available in limited quantities – may need to be downloaded from the Charity Commission website – see *Useful addresses*)

Charities: The New Law 2006 – A Practical Guide to the Charities Acts, Stephen Lloyd ed., Jordans 2007
A very thorough guide to the whole of the Charities Act 2006; includes the text of both the 2006 Act and – most importantly – the text of the Charities Act 1993 as it stands once all amendments made by the 2006 Act are included

The Charity Trustee's Handbook, Mike Eastwood, Directory of Social Change 2001

Charitable Status (6th edn), Julian Blake, Directory of Social Change 2008

The Russell-Cooke Voluntary Sector Legal Handbook (3rd edn of the *Voluntary Sector Legal Handbook*), James Sinclair Taylor, Sandy Adirondack ed., Directory of Social Change 2009

Bookkeeping and accounting in general

There is a wide range of introductory books on accounting and bookkeeping in general, which clearly explain issues such as double entry bookkeeping, methods of depreciation, cashflow forecasting and similar issues. The following are examples written for the UK context and they are suggested because they specifically focus on broader issues of financial reporting – not just bookkeeping. However, most accounting books base their examples on commercial traders and companies, and do not therefore cover charity-specific issues in any detail.

Accounting (2nd edn), Michael Jones, Wiley 2006

Accounting and Finance for Non-Specialists (5th edn), Peter Atrill and E J McLaney, FT Prentice Hall 2006

Accounting Theory and Practice (7th edn), M W E Glautier and B Underdown, Pearson Education 2006

Applied Financial Accounting and Reporting, Geoff Black, Oxford University Press 2004

Financial and Management Accounting – An Introduction (4th edn), Pauline Weetman, Pearson Education 2006

Periodicals

Charity Finance, Civil Society Media
(The main specialist journal for professionals in the charity finance field)

Charity Finance Yearbook, *Charity Finance*, Civil Society Media
(Published annually, this contains an excellent range of up to date articles and useful addresses)

Independent Examiner, Association of Charity Independent Examiners
(Aimed at independent examiners, but also covers a range of issues on accounting in smaller charities)

Most of the general periodicals aimed at the sector include regular articles on issues of financial management, and their other articles can be very useful in enabling treasurers and finance staff to keep in touch with more general developments. The following may be useful.

Third Force News, Scottish Council for Voluntary Organisations (SCVO)
(Issues for the Scottish voluntary sector)

Third Sector, Arts Publishing International

Voluntary Sector, NCVO

Caritas, Waterlow Legal and Regulatory (Caritas data)

Other government guidance

Improving Financial Relationships with the Third Sector: Guidance to Funders and Purchasers, HM Treasury Publishing Unit 2006

Financial Relationships with Third Sector Organisations: A Decision Support Tool for Public Bodies in England, National Audit Office (a web-based tool that can be found on www.nao.org.uk/guidance/better_funding)

Useful addresses

STATUTORY AND REGULATORY BODIES

Charity Commission

All enquiries should be addressed to:
Charity Commission Direct, PO Box 1227, Liverpool L69 3UG
Tel: 0845 3000 218
Website: www.charitycommission.gov.uk

Office of the Scottish Charity Regulator (OSCR)

2nd Floor, Quadrant House, 9 Riverside Drive, Dundee DD1 4NY
Tel: 01382 220446
Website: www.oscr.org.uk

Charity Commission for Northern Ireland (CCNI)

4th Floor, 24–26 Arthur Street, Belfast BT1 4GF
Tel: 028 9051 5490
Website: www.charitycommissionni.org.uk

Fundraising Standards Board (FRSB)

Hampton House, 20 Albert Embankment, London SE1 7TJ
Tel: 0845 402 5442
Website: www.frsb.org.uk

HM Revenue & Customs (Charities)

HMRC Charities, St Johns House, Merton Road, Liverpool L69 9BB
Tel: 0845 302 0203
Website: www.hmrc.gov.uk/charities

The above HMRC office now covers charities throughout the UK and should be able to assist with charity-specific issues both for direct tax issues (e.g. gift aid) and indirect taxes (e.g. VAT)

VOLUNTARY SECTOR UMBRELLA BODIES

England

National Council for Voluntary Organisations (NCVO)

Regent's Wharf, 8 All Saints Street, London N1 9RL
Helpline: 0800 2 798 798
Website: www.ncvo-vol.org.uk

The NCVO helpline can assist any charity/voluntary organisation or trustee (you do not have to be an NCVO member) with a wide range of queries and produces a range of fact sheets.

National Association for Voluntary and Community Action (NAVCA)

The Tower, 2 Furnival Square, Sheffield S1 4QL
Tel: 0114 278 6636
Website: www.navca.org.uk

Almost every district in England has a local infrastructure organisation – typically a council for voluntary service (CVS) (or equivalent) – which can offer a wide range of practical help and advice to local voluntary and community organisations. Often this includes help on managing finances and accounts; some CVSs also provide payroll services or community accounting services. The NAVCA website includes a directory to enable you to find your local CVS.

Charities Aid Foundation (CAF)

25 Kings Hill Avenue, Kings Hill, West Malling, Kent ME19 4TA
Tel: 01732 520000
Website: www.cafonline.org

CAF provides a range of support and advice for charities, including operating accounts for individuals and businesses for tax-effective giving, fundraising support, banking and investment services.

Scotland

Scottish Council for Voluntary Organisations (SCVO)

Mansfield Traquair Centre, 15 Mansfield Place, Edinburgh EH3 6BB
Information service: 0800 169 0022
Website: www.scvo.org.uk

Wales

Wales Council for Voluntary Action (WCVA)

Baltic House, Mount Stuart Square, Cardiff CF10 5FH
Helpdesk: 0800 2888 329
Website: www.wcva.org.uk

Northern Ireland

Northern Ireland Council for Voluntary Action (NICVA)

61 Duncairn Gardens, Belfast BT15 2GB
Charity advice service: 028 9087 7777
Website: www.nicva.org

PROFESSIONAL BODIES CONCERNED WITH CHARITY FINANCE

Association of Charity Independent Examiners (ACIE)

The Gatehouse, White Cross, South Road, Lancaster LA1 4XQ
Tel: 01524 348290
Website: www.acie.org.uk

Provides support, training and a qualification for independent examiners, and a referral service for charities seeking an independent examiner.

Charity Finance Directors' Group (CFDG)

3rd Floor, Downstream Building, 1 London Bridge, London SE1 9BG
Tel: 0845 345 3192
Website: www.cfdg.org.uk

Although originally established for finance directors of larger charities, CFDG now offers a range of services relevant to finance managers in a wide range of charities. CFDG is also running a project on accounting software for small to medium-sized charities.

Institute of Fundraising (IoF)

Park Place, 12 Lawn Lane, London SW8 1UD
Tel: 020 7840 1000
Website: www.institute-of-fundraising.org.uk

Although IoF members are normally fundraisers rather than treasurers and finance staff, some of the specialist groups – for example on tax-effective giving – are also of relevance to treasurers, and treasurers certainly need to be aware of the IoF's Codes of Fundraising Practice (see chapter 12).

Community Accountancy National Network (CANN)

Website: www.communityaccounting.org

CANN is the umbrella body linking community accountancy services (CASs) across the country. At the time of printing, CANN has no permanent office or staff, but the website above can be used to find a local CAS.

Groups for treasurers in specific types of charities

There are also a number of networks and associations of treasurers or finance staff within particular types of charities. If your local charity is part of a national network, contact the central office to find out if there is any specific support for local treasurers.

OTHER PROFESSIONAL BODIES

Many more general professional bodies have a charity-specialist group, including the ICAEW, ACCA, CIPFA and ICSA (see below). These bodies can also be used to help find accountants. Firms of registered auditors will always be regulated by ICAEW, ACCA, ICAS or ICAI.

Association of Accounting Technicians (AAT)

140 Aldersgate Street, London EC1A 4HY
Tel: 0845 863 0800
Website: www.aat.org.uk

Association of Chartered Certified Accountants (ACCA)

29 Lincoln's Inn Fields, London WC2A 3EE
Tel: 020 7059 5000
Website: www.acca.co.uk

Chartered Institute of Public Finance and Accountancy (CIPFA)

3 Robert Street, London WC2N 6RL
Tel: 020 7543 5600
Website: www.cipfa.org.uk

Institute of Chartered Accountants in England and Wales (ICAEW)

Chartered Accountants' Hall, PO Box 433, London EC2P 2BJ
Tel: 020 7920 8100
Website: www.icaew.co.uk

Institute of Chartered Accountants in Ireland (ICAI)

Belfast office: The Linenhall, 32–38 Linenhall Street, Belfast BT2 8BG
Tel: 028 9043 5840
Website: www.icai.ie

Institute of Chartered Accountants of Scotland (ICAS)

Chartered Accountants House, 21 Haymarket Yards, Edinburgh EH12 5BH
Tel: 0131 347 0100
Website: www.icas.org.uk

Institute of Chartered Secretaries and Administrators (ICSA)

16 Park Crescent, London W1B 1AH
Tel: 020 7580 4741
Website: www.icsa.org.uk

Index